GOODMAN'S FIVE-STAR STORIES

ADVENTURES

10 Tales of Adventure
With Exercises to Help You Read and Write

by Burton Goodman

JAMESTOWN PUBLISHERS

a division of NTC/CONTEMPORARY PUBLISHING GROUP
Lincolnwood, Illinois USA

TITLES IN THE SERIES

Editorial Director: Cynthia Krejcsi
Executive Editor: Marilyn Cunningham
Project Editor: Christine Lund Orciuch
Market Development Manager: Mary Sue Dillingofski
Cover and Interior Design: Ophelia M. Chambliss
Cover Art: Yoshi Miyake
Production Manager: Margo Goia

Acknowledgments are on page 140, which is to be considered an extension of
this copyright page.

ISBN: 0-89061-874-7

Published by Jamestown Publishers,
a division of NTC/Contemporary Publishing Group, Inc.,
4255 West Touhy Avenue,
Lincolnwood (Chicago), Illinois 60712-1975 U.S.A.
© 1998 by Burton Goodman.

7 8 9 10 11 12 13 14 15 16 17 18 19 20 100/108 09 08 07 06 05 04 03

Contents

To the Student

Here are ten exciting Adventures. I have picked these stories because I like them very much. I think that you will like them too. They are tales that come from around the world.

These tales will be fun to read. And the exercises will be fun to do too. They will help you read and write better. And you will learn some important literature skills.

Study the vocabulary words before you read the story. They will help you understand the story. Later, do the exercises after each of the TALES:

TELL ABOUT THE STORY

ADD WORDS TO SENTENCES

LEARN NEW WORDS

EXPLAIN WHAT HAPPENED

SPOT STORY ELEMENTS

TELL ABOUT THE STORY helps you find key facts in a story. Sometimes these facts are called *details.*

ADD WORDS TO SENTENCES builds your reading and vocabulary skills. This part uses fill-in, or cloze, exercises.

LEARN NEW WORDS builds your vocabulary skills. Often, you can work out the meaning of a new word. You can do this by looking at the words *around* the new word. When you do this, you are using *context clues.* The vocabulary words in each story are printed in **dark type.** You may look back at these words when you answer the vocabulary questions.

EXPLAIN WHAT HAPPENED builds your *critical thinking* skills. You will have to think about what happened in the story. Then you must figure out the answers.

SPOT STORY ELEMENTS helps you understand some important elements of literature. Some story elements are *plot, character,* and *setting.* On page 3 you will find the meanings of these words. You may look back at the meanings when you answer the questions.

Another part, **THINK SOME MORE ABOUT THE STORY** gives you a chance to think, talk, and *write* about the story.

There are four questions for each of the **TALES** exercises. Here is the way to do the exercises:

- Do all the exercises.

- Check your answers with your teacher.

- Use the scoring chart at the end of each exercise to figure out your score for that exercise. Give yourself 5 points for each right answer. (Since there are four questions, you can get up to 20 points for each exercise.)

- Use the **TALES** scoring chart at the end of the exercises to add up your total score. If you get all the questions right, your score will be 100.

- Keep track of how well you do. First write your Total Score on the **Progress Chart** on page 138. Then write your score on the **Progress Graph** on page 139. Look at the **Progress Graph** to see how much you improve.

I know that you will like reading the stories in this book. And the exercises after the **TALES** will help you read and write better.

Now . . . get ready for some *Adventures.*

Burton Goodman

The Short Story—
Important Words

Character: a character is someone in a story. The writer tells you what the character is like. The way a character looks, speaks, and acts *characterizes* that person.

Main Character: the person the story is mostly about.

Plot: what happens in a story. The first thing that takes place in a story is the first thing in the *plot*. The last thing that takes place in the story is the last thing in the plot.

Setting: where and when the story takes place. The *setting* is the time and the place of the story.

1

The Day It Snowed Tortillas

by Joe Hayes

Before You Read

Before you read "The Day It Snowed Tortillas," study the words below. Make sure you know what each word means. This will help you understand the story.

pancakes: thin, flat cakes made of flour, milk, and eggs

squeeze: push to make something fit into

alphabet: the letters used to make words

copy: to write something so that it looks just like something else

expected: thought that something would happen

fool: someone who acts in a silly way

crazy: saying or doing strange things

The Day It Snowed Tortillas

by Joe Hayes

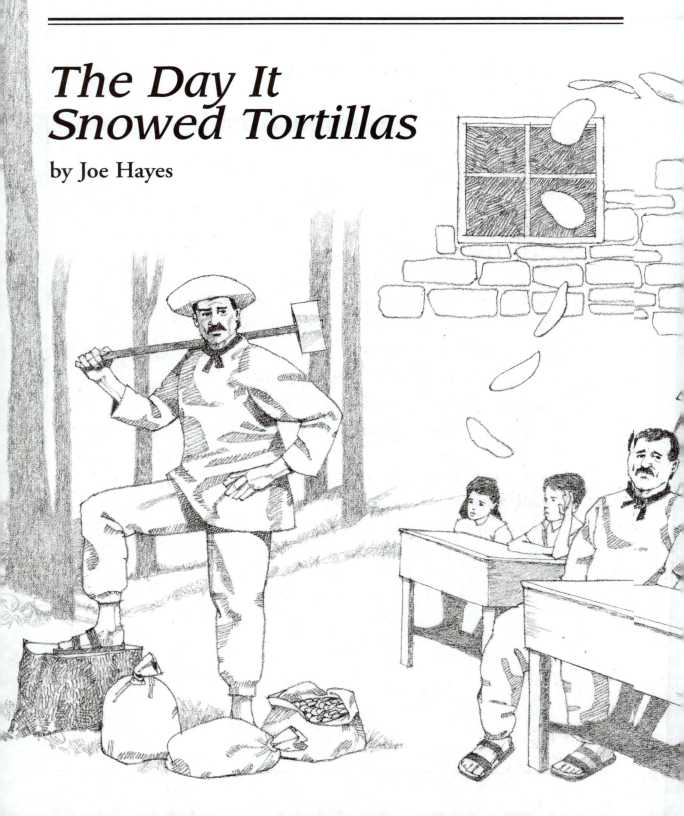

This story is about a woodcutter. He was good at his work. He cut down big trees. Then he **chopped** the trees into firewood. He sold the firewood in the village. He made a good living

The woodcutter never went to school. He could not read or write. He was not very smart. He was always doing **foolish** things. But the woodcutter was lucky. He had a very clever wife. She always got him out of trouble.

One day the woodcutter was in the forest. He was working. It began to get dark. So he started for home.

On the way there, he **noticed** three bags. They were by the side of the road.

The woodcutter picked up the first bag. He looked inside. It was filled with pieces of gold. He looked into the second bag. It was full of gold too. And so was the third.

He loaded the bags onto his donkey. Then he took them home to show his wife.

His wife saw that the bags were filled with gold. She was very surprised.

"Listen to me," she said. "Do not tell *anyone* that you found this gold! It must belong to some robbers. They probably hid it in the forest. If they find out we have this gold, they will come here. They will kill us! They will take back the gold."

Then she thought to herself, "I know my husband. He can never keep a secret. He may talk about the gold. What should I do?"

She thought of a plan. She told her husband, "You must do something right now. Go into the village. Bring back some large **sacks** of flour. I need a lot of flour. Bring back a hundred pounds of flour."

The woodcutter went off to the village. He was not happy about going. He said to himself, "I worked in the forest all day. Now I must bring back a hundred pounds of flour. I am tired of all this work."

He went to a store and bought the flour. He brought it home to his wife.

"Thank you," she said. "Thank you very much. You have worked very hard. You must be tired. Why don't you lie down for a while?"

The woodcutter liked that idea. He lay down on the bed. Soon he fell fast asleep.

The woman waited until her husband was asleep. Then she went to work. She took the flour. She began to make tortillas. Tortillas are thin, flat cakes. They look a little like pancakes. They are good to eat.

She kept making tortillas. She made more and more tortillas. They filled up the whole kitchen. She used up the hundred pounds of flour. She made piles and piles of tortillas.

Then she took the tortillas outside. She threw them all over the ground.

The woodcutter was very tired. He slept all that evening. He slept through the night. He did not wake up until the next morning.

The woodcutter got up. He stepped outside. He saw that the ground was covered with tortillas. He called to his wife. "What happened here? What does this mean?"

His wife went to the door. She looked outside. She said, "Oh, dear! It must have snowed tortillas last night!"

"Snowed tortillas?" said the man. "I never heard of such a thing."

"What?" she answered. "You never heard of it snowing tortillas? Well! You never went to school. There are a lot of things you do not know. You better go to school. There are some things you must learn."

So she made him some lunch. She put it into a bag. Then she made him go off to the school.

The woodcutter got to the school a little later. But he did not know how to read. He did not know how to write. So they put him in the first grade. He had to squeeze into a chair. The chair was too small for him. It was made for a child. It was hard for him to sit.

Then the teacher asked questions. The children raised their hands. The children answered the questions. The woodcutter could not answer any of the questions.

He had to go to the blackboard to write. But he did not know the alphabet. A little boy was standing next to him. The boy wrote his name on the board. The woodcutter tried to copy what the little boy wrote. The woodcutter wrote the boy's name. The other children saw that the man was writing the boy's name. He was not writing his own. They began to laugh.

The woodcutter could not stand it any longer. He rushed out of the school. He hurried home. He told his wife, "I have had enough school. I am going to work. I am going to cut firewood."

"Fine," she called after him. "You go do your work."

A week later, the robbers came to the woodcutter's house. His wife was not surprised. She thought that they would come. She expected them.

The robbers were very angry. They said to the woman, "Where is the gold that your husband found?"

The woman shook her head. She looked surprised. "Gold?" she said. "I do not know what you mean. I do not know anything about any gold."

"Come on!" the robbers said. "Your husband has been talking to everyone in the village. He said that he found three bags of gold. Those bags belong to us. You better give them back!"

The woman shook her head again. She asked, "Did my husband say that? Oh, that poor man! I do not know what to do about him. He says the strangest things. I do not know anything about your gold."

"We will see," said the robbers. "We will find out soon enough. We will wait here until he comes home." So the robbers waited around all day. While they waited, they cleaned their guns.

Toward evening, the woodcutter came up the path with his donkey. The robbers ran out. They grabbed the man. They began to shake him.

They asked, "Where is the gold you found? You better tell us! You better tell us right away!"

The woodcutter thought for a moment. "Gold?" he said. "Oh, yes. Now I remember. My wife hid the gold."

He called out, "Wife. What did you do with that gold?"

His wife looked very surprised. "What gold?" she said. "I do not know what you are talking about."

"Sure you do. Don't you remember? I brought home three bags of gold. It was the day before it snowed tortillas. Remember? It snowed tortillas all night. And in the morning, you sent me to school."

The robbers looked at each other.

They said, "Did he say that it snowed tortillas? Did he say that she sent him to school?"

They sadly shook their heads. "Why are we wasting our time? This man is a fool. He does not know what he is talking about."

So they went away. They thought that the woodcutter was crazy. They did not believe a word that he said.

From that day on, it did not matter if the woodcutter was smart. It did not even matter if he was a good woodcutter. For he was a rich man. He and his wife had the gold all to themselves. And the three robbers never came back.

TELL ABOUT THE STORY.

Put an *x* in the box next to the right answer. Each sentence tells a *fact* about the story.

1. The woodcutter was
   - ☐ a. very weak.
   - ☐ b. very strong.
   - ☐ c. very smart.

2. The wife told the woodcutter to bring back
   - ☐ a. more wood.
   - ☐ b. some tortillas.
   - ☐ c. a hundred pounds of flour.

3. At school the woodcutter
   - ☐ a. read a story.
   - ☐ b. answered many questions.
   - ☐ c. could not answer any questions.

4. The robbers came to the house to
   - ☐ a. get their gold.
   - ☐ b. eat dinner.
   - ☐ c. buy firewood.

ADD WORDS TO SENTENCES.

Complete the sentences below. Fill in each blank with one of the words in the box. Each word can be found in the story. There are five words and four blanks. This means that one word in the box will not be used.

In 1848 gold was _____ in
$_1$
California. People hurried there from everywhere, hoping to find

_____. San Francisco was
$_2$

just a _____ town in 1848.
$_3$

By 1849 it _____ become a
$_4$

growing city.

gold		small
	idea	
found		had

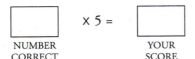

NUMBER CORRECT × 5 = YOUR SCORE

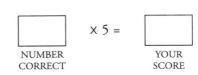

NUMBER CORRECT × 5 = YOUR SCORE

13

LEARN NEW WORDS.

The vocabulary words are printed in **dark type** in the story. You may look back at the words before you answer these questions. Put an *x* in the box next to the right answer.

1. He chopped the trees into fire wood. The word *chopped* means
   - ☐ a. cut.
   - ☐ b. climbed.
   - ☐ c. sold.

2. The woodcutter did foolish things and got into trouble. The word *foolish* means
   - ☐ a. good.
   - ☐ b. wise.
   - ☐ c. silly.

3. He noticed three bags by the side of the road. The word *noticed* means
   - ☐ a. saw.
   - ☐ b. wanted.
   - ☐ c. lost.

4. The woodcutter bought some large sacks of flour. What are *sacks*?
   - ☐ a. boxes
   - ☐ b. bags
   - ☐ c. cakes

☐ x 5 = ☐

NUMBER
CORRECT

YOUR
SCORE

EXPLAIN WHAT HAPPENED.

Here is how to answer these questions. First think about what happened in the story. Then *figure out* (work out) the right answer. This is called *critical thinking*.

1. The wife was afraid that her husband would
   - ☐ a. spend the gold.
   - ☐ b. give away the gold.
   - ☐ c. tell people about the gold.

2. How many tortillas did the woman make?
   - ☐ a. She made one or two.
   - ☐ b. She may just a few.
   - ☐ c. She made many.

3. Why did the woodcutter hurry out of the school?
   - ☐ a. He did not like it there.
   - ☐ b. He left his lunch at home.
   - ☐ c. The teacher said to go home.

4. Why did the robbers think the woodcutter was a fool?
   - ☐ a. He said his wife hid the gold.
   - ☐ b. He said it snowed tortillas.
   - ☐ c. They talked to his teacher.

☐ x 5 = ☐

NUMBER
CORRECT

YOUR
SCORE

SPOT STORY ELEMENTS.

Some story elements are **plot, character,** and **setting.** (See page 3.) Put an *x* in the box next to the right answer.

1. What happened first in the *plot*?
   - [ ] a. The woodcutter went to the school.
   - [ ] b. The woodcutter found three bags of gold.
   - [ ] c. The woodcutter bought the flour.

2. What happened last in the *plot*?
   - [ ] a. The robbers came to the house.
   - [ ] b. The woodcutter fell asleep.
   - [ ] c. The woman made tortillas.

3. Which word best describes (tells about) the *character* of the wife?
   - [ ] a. angry
   - [ ] b. clever
   - [ ] c. sad

4. Which sentence best describes the *character* of the woodcutter?
   - [ ] a. He was lazy.
   - [ ] b. He could read well.
   - [ ] c. He was strong, but not smart.

[   ] x 5 = [   ]

NUMBER CORRECT   YOUR SCORE

THINK SOME MORE ABOUT THE STORY.

Your teacher might want you to write your answers.
- Why did the woman make tortillas and then throw them on the ground?
- Show that the woman knew her husband very well.
- Suppose that the robbers did not believe that the husband was a fool. How do you think the story would have ended?

Write your scores in the boxes below. Then write your scores on pages 138 and 139.

[   ] + **T**ELL ABOUT THE STORY

[   ] + **A**DD WORDS TO SENTENCES

[   ] + **L**EARN NEW WORDS

[   ] + **E**XPLAIN WHAT HAPPENED

[   ] = **S**POT STORY ELEMENTS

[   ] TOTAL SCORE: Story 1

2
The Captain

based on a story by Leo Tolstoy

Before You Read

Before you read "The Captain," study the words below.
Make sure you know what each word means. This will
help you understand the story.

ship: a large boat

sailor: someone who works on a ship

dock: a landing place where ships are tied up. Most docks
are made of wood and are at the edge of the water.

deck: the floor of a ship

mast (of a ship): a pole (a tall piece of wood) that holds
the sails

beam: a long, heavy piece of wood

narrow: not wide

The Captain

based on a story by Leo Tolstoy

Ivan lived in a small village. It was near the sea. From his window Ivan saw many ships. Ivan loved ships. He loved the sea.

Ivan wanted to be a sailor. His father was a sailor. His father was the captain of a ship.

One morning Ivan came down to breakfast. His mother and father were at the table. They were talking. His father had just come back from a long **voyage.** He had been away for two months.

His father said, "Sonia, I have been thinking. In two weeks Ivan's school will be closed. It will be vacation time. I must go back to sea then. Perhaps Ivan could come with me. This will not be a long trip."

Ivan's heart **leaped** with joy. He wanted to go with his father. He wanted to go very much. He hoped that his mother would say yes.

But Ivan's mother did not answer. She looked worried. She said, "I do not know. Ivan is still a boy. The sea is no place for a boy."

Ivan's father laughed. He said, "That is so. But Ivan is twelve years old now. He can take care of himself. He will be fine."

"I do not know," answered his mother. She was quiet for a long time.

Ivan spoke up. "Please, mother," he said.

She looked at her son. "All right," she finally said. "You may go."

Ivan could hardly wait. At last the big day came. Ivan and his father took their things. They went down to the dock. They got on a big ship.

Ivan felt very proud. His father was not a tall man. But he was very strong. And he had a loud voice. He told the sailors what to do. The sailors listened to him.

They said, "Yes, Captain. Right away, Captain. I will do that at once." Then they hurried away.

At home Ivan's father often laughed. But on the ship he never smiled. He was *the captain*. He marched around the ship. He made sure that the sailors did their jobs. He made sure that everything went well.

It was a very **pleasant** trip. Ivan liked it very much. The sailors knew he was the captain's son. Everyone was very nice to him.

The ship was on its way home. It was a sunny day. Many sailors were on deck. They were feeling good. They knew that they would be home soon.

A monkey jumped onto the deck. The monkey was a sailor's pet. The sailors clapped their hands. The monkey danced around.

The monkey suddenly grabbed Ivan's hat. She put it on her head. All of the sailors laughed. The monkey ran across the deck.

Ivan shouted, "Give me back my hat!" The monkey took off Ivan's hat. She waved it in the air. The sailors laughed again. The monkey hopped over to the mast.

Ivan was angry. He ran toward the mast. The monkey jumped onto the mast. She began to climb up the mast. It was very tall. The monkey climbed up to a wooden beam. She sat down on the beam. Then she smiled down at the boy.

A rope ladder hung down from the mast. Ivan grabbed the ladder. He began to climb. He climbed up to the wooden beam. He reached out to grab his hat. But the monkey jumped away. She hopped onto the mast.

The monkey began to climb again. She climbed up to the second beam. She sat down on the beam. Again she smiled at the boy.

All of the sailors watched. They were having a good time. They thought this was fun.

Ivan climbed up to the second beam. He reached out to grab his hat. Again the monkey ran away. She hopped onto the beam. Quickly she began to climb. The monkey climbed and climbed. She climbed up to the top of the tall mast.

Then the monkey dropped the hat. It landed a few feet away. It landed on a beam. The beam was very high! It was sixty feet above the deck!

Ivan looked up. He saw the hat on the beam. It was far above his head.

Ivan kept looking at the hat. Then he saw the monkey on the mast. She was smiling down at him. Slowly, Ivan began to climb.

Ivan climbed up to the beam. Then he stepped onto the beam. He took two steps. The hat was at the end of the beam. It was twenty feet away.

Ivan walked very slowly along the beam. The beam was only one foot wide!

The sailors on the deck looked up. They watched the captain's son. They were no longer having fun. Their hearts were filled with fear. The beam was narrow. It was very high. The boy might **slip.** What if he fell? He would hit the deck below! He would be killed at once!

The sailors did not move. They did not speak. All eyes were on the captain's son.

The boy took another step. One sailor could not stop himself. He suddenly yelled, *"Watch out! Look out!"*

Ivan heard the call. His eyes were on the hat. But now he looked down. He saw how high he was. He did not know he was that high! The boy began to shake. He could not move!

Just then the captain came onto the deck. He saw the sailors. They were looking up. The captain saw his son. The boy was shaking. He might fall to the deck!

The captain turned at once. He hurried to his room. He came back with a gun. It was a hunting rifle.

He pointed the rifle at his son. *"Jump into the water! Jump! Jump or I'll shoot!"* the captain shouted.

Ivan looked down. He did not understand.

"Jump into the water—or I'll shoot!" the father called again.

The boy kept shaking on the beam.

"I will count to three!" the father yelled.

As he was saying "Three," the boy jumped out into the sea.

Ivan hit the water. He went down. Ten sailors jumped into the sea. They pulled Ivan out. They dragged him to the ship.

A minute later Ivan made a sound. Water came out of his mouth. He shook his head. He slowly looked around.

The captain knew that his son was all right. The captain quickly turned away. He hurried back to his room. He did not want anyone to see his face. He did not want anyone to see him crying.

TELL ABOUT THE STORY.

Put an *x* in the box next to the right answer. Each sentence tells a *fact* about the story.

1. Ivan was
   - ☐ a. ten years old.
   - ☐ b. twelve years old.
   - ☐ c. fourteen years old.

2. Ivan lived in a village that was
   - ☐ a. on top of a mountain.
   - ☐ b. in a valley.
   - ☐ c. near the sea.

3. The monkey grabbed Ivan's
   - ☐ a. hat.
   - ☐ b. gloves.
   - ☐ c. coat.

4. The captain told Ivan to
   - ☐ a. be careful.
   - ☐ b. come down at once.
   - ☐ c. jump into the water.

ADD WORDS TO SENTENCES.

Complete the sentences below. Fill in each blank with one of the words in the box. Each word can be found in the story. There are five words and four blanks. This means that one word in the box will not be used.

The *Titanic* was once the biggest

_____ in the world. Everyone
      1

thought it could _____ sink.
                        2

But on its first _____, it hit a
                       3

large piece of ice. Three hours later,

the ship fell to the bottom of the

_____.
      4

never	ship
	sea
climb	voyage

☐ x 5 = ☐

NUMBER CORRECT   YOUR SCORE

☐ x 5 = ☐

NUMBER CORRECT   YOUR SCORE

25

LEARN NEW WORDS.

The vocabulary words are printed in **dark type** in the story. You may look back at the words before you answer these questions. Put an *x* in the box next to the right answer.

1. His father came back from a long sea voyage. A *voyage* is a
   - [ ] a. boat.
   - [ ] b. meal.
   - [ ] c. trip.

2. Ivan's heart leaped with joy. The word *leaped* means
   - [ ] a. jumped.
   - [ ] b. stopped.
   - [ ] c. wondered.

3. It was a pleasant trip. Ivan liked it very much. Something that is *pleasant* is
   - [ ] a. hard.
   - [ ] b. slow.
   - [ ] c. fun.

4. The sailors were afraid that Ivan might slip. The word *slip* means
   - [ ] a. to laugh.
   - [ ] b. to fall.
   - [ ] c. to yell.

```
┌──────┐          ┌──────┐
│      │  X 5 =   │      │
└──────┘          └──────┘
NUMBER            YOUR
CORRECT           SCORE
```

EXPLAIN WHAT HAPPENED.

Here is how to answer these questions. First think about what happened in the story. Then *figure out* (work out) the right answer. This is called *critical thinking.*

1. Which sentence is true?
   - [ ] a. Ivan was afraid to go to sea.
   - [ ] b. Ivan did not like boats.
   - [ ] c. Ivan's mother thought Ivan was too young to go to sea.

2. Ivan probably kept climbing after his hat because
   - [ ] a. the sailors made him do it.
   - [ ] b. the hat cost a lot of money.
   - [ ] c. he was angry with the monkey.

3. The story shows that Ivan's father
   - [ ] a. did not care about Ivan.
   - [ ] b. could think very quickly.
   - [ ] c. did not like his job.

4. Why did the captain make Ivan jump into the water?
   - [ ] a. to show that Ivan would listen to him
   - [ ] b. to keep Ivan from falling onto the deck
   - [ ] c. to teach Ivan to swim

```
┌──────┐          ┌──────┐
│      │  X 5 =   │      │
└──────┘          └──────┘
NUMBER            YOUR
CORRECT           SCORE
```

SPOT STORY ELEMENTS.

Some story elements are **plot**, **character**, and **setting**. (See page 3.) Put an *x* in the box next to the right answer.

1. What happened first in the *plot*?
   - ☐ a. Ivan jumped into the sea.
   - ☐ b. Ivan had breakfast with his parents.
   - ☐ c. The sailors watched Ivan climb the ladder.

2. What happened last in the *plot*?
   - ☐ a. The captain pointed the rifle at Ivan.
   - ☐ b. Ivan ran after the monkey.
   - ☐ c. Ivan and his father got on the ship.

3. Which sentence best *characterizes* (tells about) Ivan's father?
   - ☐ a. He was very tall.
   - ☐ b. He was not strong.
   - ☐ c. He was strong and had a loud voice.

4. The story is *set*
   - ☐ a. in a school.
   - ☐ b. on a ship.
   - ☐ c. in Ivan's room.

☐ × 5 = ☐

NUMBER CORRECT   YOUR SCORE

THINK SOME MORE ABOUT THE STORY.

Your teacher might want you to write your answers.

- At home Ivan's father often laughed. But on the ship he never smiled. Why do you think he was different on the ship?
- The captain did not want anyone to see him cry. Why? Do you think he was right to feel that way? Explain.
- Suppose that Ivan's father had not made him jump into the water. How do you think the story would have ended?

Write your scores in the boxes below. Then write your scores on pages 138 and 139.

☐ **T**ELL ABOUT THE STORY
\+
☐ **A**DD WORDS TO SENTENCES
\+
☐ **L**EARN NEW WORDS
\+
☐ **E**XPLAIN WHAT HAPPENED
\+
☐ **S**POT STORY ELEMENTS
=
☐ TOTAL SCORE: Story 2

3
The Visitors

by George Shea

Before You Read

Before you read "The Visitors," study the words below. Make sure you know what each word means. This will help you understand the story.

creatures: living people and animals

floated: moved slowly in the air

forward: ahead; to the front

planet: Planets move around the sun. Some planets are bigger than Earth.

fooling around: telling jokes; having fun

The Visitors

by George Shea

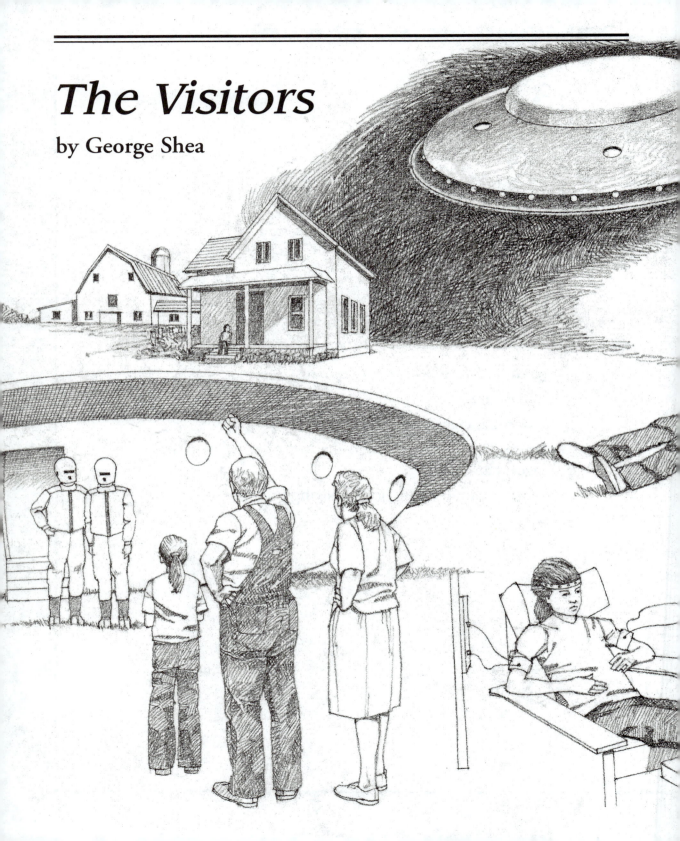

It was lonely on the farm. There wasn't much to do. Pate sat on the back steps of her house. She looked up at the sky. "There are so many stars up there," she thought to herself.

Pate noticed one star. It was very bright. It was the biggest star in the sky. Suddenly, the star began to get bigger. It got bigger and bigger. It got brighter and brighter.

Pate could not move. She couldn't even cry out. She could not believe what she saw. She just kept **staring** up. The whole sky filled with light!

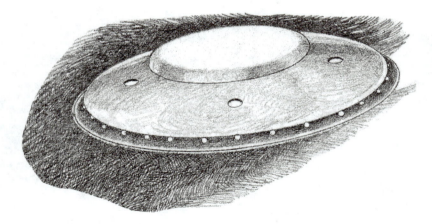

Then she saw a large round spaceship. It was about 100 feet wide. It had orange lights. They blinked on and off.

The ship was coming down! It was landing in the backyard!

Pate's parents came out of the house. They stood in the yard. They did not speak. They seemed afraid.

The ship landed. A door in its side suddenly opened. Two creatures came out. They floated in the air. Then they landed softly on the ground.

Pate was surprised. She thought to herself, "They look just like us."

One of the creatures spoke. It said to her, "Come closer to the ship. We will not **harm** you."

"No!" said her father. "Do not move! Stay where you are, Pate!"

The creature moved toward Pate. Her father stepped forward. He stood between Pate and the creature.

"Do not touch her," he said. Then he **raised** his arm.

The other creature moved behind Pate's father. It put something against the back of his neck.

Pate's father fell to the ground. Pate and her mother ran to where he was lying. They were afraid he was dead.

"He lives. He is fine," said the first creature. "He will wake up in an hour. He will not remember this."

Suddenly, the other creature was behind Pate's mother. It **pressed** something against her neck. She fell to the ground too.

Pate looked down at her mother. Pate could see that her mother was breathing. She saw that her father was breathing too.

"Come with us, please," said the first creature. "Come into the ship. We need to test you."

"Test me?" said Pate. "What do you mean? Why me?"

"You are young. We have already tested others on your planet. But all of them were older. Do not be afraid. We will not hurt you. You will be back with your parents very soon."

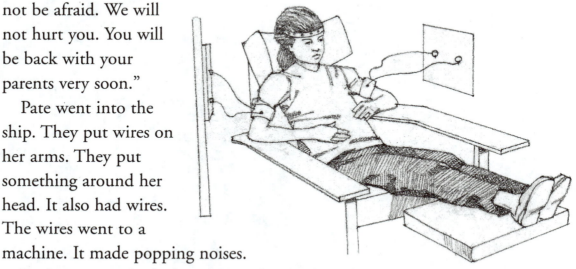

Pate went into the ship. They put wires on her arms. They put something around her head. It also had wires. The wires went to a machine. It made popping noises.

Both creatures looked at the machine. Then they asked Pate questions. They asked her about her school. They asked her what she learned there.

Pate answered their questions. Then she said, "Why do you want to know these things?"

One of them said, "It is our job. Our people must know what is happening on other planets. Someday we may talk to the people who run your country. But we will be friends. We will not hurt your people."

"Where are you from?" Pate asked.

"A planet," one of them said. "Its name does not matter."

"We are finished now," one of them said.

Pate felt something against the back of her neck. Then everything went black.

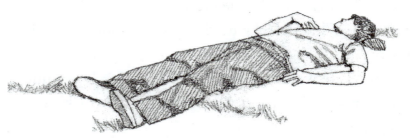

Pate woke up an hour later. She was lying on the ground in the backyard. Her parents were standing over her. They looked very worried.

"Pate. Are you all right?" her mother asked.

"I—I think so," said Pate. She slowly got to her feet. "What happened?" she asked.

"We do not know," said her father. "You probably fell down. We found you lying here. We must have fallen too. That is strange. It is very strange. Do you remember what happened?"

Pate looked around the yard. Everything seemed the same. Nothing had changed.

"No," she said. "I do not remember anything."

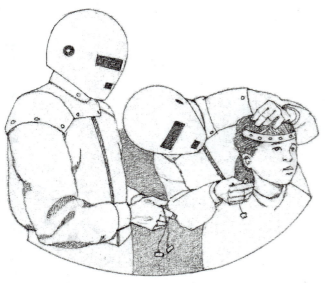

Weeks went by. Then one night Pate had a dream. She dreamed about the ship. She saw the faces of the creatures. She saw them put wires on her arms. She saw them put something around her head. She saw the machine. It made popping noises.

In the dream Pate heard the creatures' questions again. They asked, "What do they teach you in school? What do you learn?"

Suddenly Pate woke up. She began to shake. Everything in the dream seemed so *real*. She looked at the clock. It was time to get up.

Pate ate breakfast. Then she went to school. That morning her teacher, Mr. Anyo, talked about life in space.

He asked the class, "Does anyone believe that there is life on other planets?"

Suddenly, Pate remembered everything. She was sure that what she had dreamed had really happened. She raised her hand.

"I do!" she said. "I saw a spaceship. That was just a few weeks ago. It landed in my backyard."

The whole class laughed. Mr. Anyo laughed too. "That's very funny, Pate," he said. "Now let's stop fooling around."

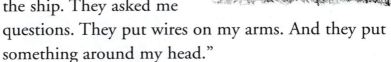

"No! No! I am telling the truth!" Pate said. "The spaceship landed in my backyard. Two creatures came out of the ship. They took me inside the ship. They asked me questions. They put wires on my arms. And they put something around my head."

"Someone ought to look *inside* your head!" a kid yelled out. Everyone laughed.

Pate stood up. "But it's true!" she said. "It is true! It is true!"

"Pate. Please sit down," said Mr. Anyo. "You must stop this talk! If you do not, I will have to send you to THE PLACE FOR PEOPLE WHO NEED HELP."

Pate did not sit down. She ran to the board. "But it's all true!" she said. "It is true! It is true! I remember it all! I remember their spaceship. There were some words on its side. I could not tell what they said. They looked like this." She wrote something on the board.

Mr. Anyo was moving toward her.

Pate went on. "And next to the words was a little picture. It was red, white, and blue. The little picture had red and white stripes. And there were stars in a corner of the picture. There were fifty stars. I counted them all. And there were letters near the picture. They said U.S.A."

Pate drew the little picture.

"See?" she said.

A little later Mr. Anyo sent Pate to THE PLACE FOR PEOPLE WHO NEED HELP.

TELL ABOUT THE STORY.

Put an *x* in the box next to the right answer. Each sentence tells a *fact* about the story.

1. The spaceship landed
   - ☐ a. on top of the house.
   - ☐ b. near the school.
   - ☐ c. in Pate's backyard.

2. The creatures said they wanted to
   - ☐ a. test Pate.
   - ☐ b. take Pate away.
   - ☐ c. speak to Pate's teacher.

3. Pate remembered the creatures when she
   - ☐ a. read a story about them.
   - ☐ b. saw a movie about them.
   - ☐ c. dreamed about them.

4. When Pate told the class what had happened to her, everyone
   - ☐ a. laughed.
   - ☐ b. believed her story.
   - ☐ c. asked her questions.

ADD WORDS TO SENTENCES.

Complete the sentences below. Fill in each blank with one of the words in the box. Each word can be found in the story. There are five words and four blanks. This means that one word in the box will not be used.

Suppose you told a friend that you saw a _____ land. Do you
1

think that your _____ would
2

believe what you said? Suppose a friend said that *she* saw a spaceship

_____. Do you think that you
3

would _____ your friend?
4

friend	believe
dream	
spaceship	land

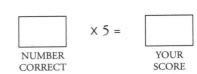

NUMBER CORRECT ☐ × 5 = ☐ YOUR SCORE

NUMBER CORRECT ☐ × 5 = ☐ YOUR SCORE

LEARN NEW WORDS.

The vocabulary words are printed in **dark type** in the story. You may look back at the words before you answer these questions. Put an *x* in the box next to the right answer.

1. Pate kept staring up at the sky. The word *staring* means
   - ☐ a. crying.
   - ☐ b. looking.
   - ☐ c. waving.

2. The creature said, "We will not harm you." The word *harm* means
   - ☐ a. leave.
   - ☐ b. hurt.
   - ☐ c. help.

3. Pate raised her hand to answer the question. The word *raised* means
   - ☐ a. used.
   - ☐ b. hit.
   - ☐ c. put up.

4. The creature pressed something against Pate's neck. The word *pressed* means
   - ☐ a. pushed.
   - ☐ b. threw.
   - ☐ c. needed.

☐ X 5 = ☐

NUMBER CORRECT   YOUR SCORE

EXPLAIN WHAT HAPPENED.

Here is how to answer these questions. First think about what happened in the story. Then *figure out* (work out) the right answer. This is called *critical thinking*.

1. We may infer (figure out) that the creatures came from
   - ☐ a. Earth.
   - ☐ b. the moon.
   - ☐ c. the sun.

2. Pate must have lived somewhere
   - ☐ a. in the United States.
   - ☐ b. where everyone was kind.
   - ☐ c. where the people had never heard of the U.S.A.

3. Mr. Anyo thought that
   - ☐ a. Pate's story was true.
   - ☐ b. there was something wrong with Pate.
   - ☐ c. creatures lived on other planets.

4. What did Pate draw on the board?
   - ☐ a. the faces of the creatures
   - ☐ b. a machine that made popping noises
   - ☐ c. a picture of the American flag

☐ X 5 = ☐

NUMBER CORRECT   YOUR SCORE

40

SPOT STORY ELEMENTS.

Some story elements are **plot**, **character**, and **setting**. (See page 3.) Put an *x* in the box next to the right answer.

1. What happened first in the *plot*?
   - ☐ a. The creatures put wires on Pate's arm.
   - ☐ b. Pate saw a very bright star in the sky.
   - ☐ c. Pate told the class she saw a spaceship.

2. What happened last in the *plot*?
   - ☐ a. Mr. Anyo sent Pate to THE PLACE FOR PEOPLE WHO NEED HELP.
   - ☐ b. The spaceship landed.
   - ☐ c. Mr. Anyo told Pate to stop fooling around.

3. Who is the *main character* in the story?
   - ☐ a. Mr. Anyo
   - ☐ b. Pate
   - ☐ c. a creature

4. The end of the story is *set*
   - ☐ a. in Pate's house.
   - ☐ b. in a spaceship.
   - ☐ c. at Pate's school.

☐ x 5 = ☐

NUMBER CORRECT   YOUR SCORE

THINK SOME MORE ABOUT THE STORY.

Your teacher might want you to write your answers.

- Do you think you would like to live in the place where Pate lived? Why?
- Explain why Pate was sent to THE PLACE FOR PEOPLE WHO NEED HELP.
- Did you think the story was funny or sad—or both? Tell why.
- Did the ending of the story surprise you? Explain.

Write your scores in the boxes below. Then write your scores on pages 138 and 139.

☐ **T**ELL ABOUT THE STORY
+
☐ **A**DD WORDS TO SENTENCES
+
☐ **L**EARN NEW WORDS
+
☐ **E**XPLAIN WHAT HAPPENED
+
☐ **S**POT STORY ELEMENTS
=
☐ TOTAL SCORE: Story 3

4
King Midas and the Golden Touch

from a Greek myth by Nathaniel Hawthorne

Before You Read

Before you read "King Midas and the Golden Touch," study the words below. Make sure you know what each word means. This will help you understand the story.

myth: an old story; a story from the past

treasure: gold, money, or other things that are important to someone

palace: the home of a king or queen

satisfied: made happy; pleased

indeed: really; something that is so

shines: is bright with light

King Midas and the Golden Touch

from a Greek myth by Nathaniel Hawthorne

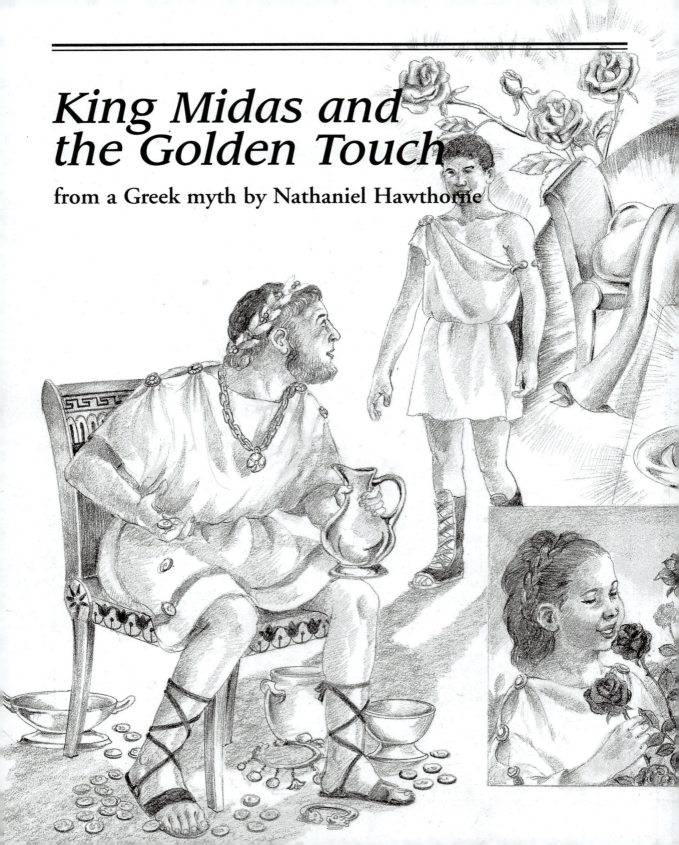

A long time ago there lived a king named Midas. King Midas loved gold. He loved gold very much. There was only one thing he loved more. That was his little daughter, Marygold.

King Midas had once loved flowers. He had planted a garden filled with roses. The garden still grew. The roses were beautiful.

Sometimes Midas went into his garden. He looked at the roses. He said to himself, "There are so many roses in my garden. I wish each rose were made of gold. Oh, how wonderful my garden would be."

King Midas lived in a very large palace. It had many rooms. The biggest room in the palace was filled with gold. Midas called it his treasure room.

Every day Midas went to that room. He counted his bags of gold. He let the pieces of gold slip through his fingers. Then he whispered softly, "Oh, Midas! Rich King Midas! What a happy man you are!" Then he whispered again, "But how much happier you would be if you had more gold!"

One day Midas was in his treasure room. He was counting his gold. Suddenly a shadow fell over the gold. King Midas looked up. He saw a young man. The young man had a smile on his face.

King Midas was sure he had locked the door. No one could break into that room. So the king knew that the man must have very great powers.

The young man smiled again. He had a very kind smile. Midas thought, "Should I be afraid of this man? No. He is friendly. See how he smiles. Has he come here to help me?"

The man looked around. Then he said, "You are rich, King Midas. You are very, very rich. No other room in the world has this much gold."

"I have done well," Midas said. "Very well. That is so. But it has taken me years to get this gold. And there is so much more gold I would like to have."

"What?" said the young man. "You are not satisfied?"

"I am not," said the king.

"Tell me," asked the young man. "What would satisfy you? I would like to know."

King Midas thought for a while. Then he said. "It is this. Only this. I wish—that everything I touch would turn to gold."

The young man smiled. "The Golden Touch!" he said. "The Golden Touch! That is a very fine wish. A fine wish, indeed! But are you sure that would satisfy you? Would that make you happy?"

"Oh, yes!" said the king. "I am sure of that!"

"And you would never be sorry because of it?"

"Sorry? Oh, never!" King Midas said.

"You shall have your wish," the young man said. "You shall have your wish when the sun comes up. Everything you touch will turn to gold."

King Midas smiled. He was filled with joy.

"Good-bye—for now," the young man said. And he **disappeared.**

Midas woke up early the next morning. The sun was not up yet. Midas thought about the young man. Had it all been a dream? No! The young man had really been there!

Midas reached out. He touched a chair. Then he touched the table by his bed. They did not change. They did not turn to gold!

Midas walked to the window. He looked outside. The morning was gray. Then he saw the sun. It was just coming up.

Midas walked to the bed. He touched the bed. It turned to gold! He picked up a book. It turned to gold! He put on his clothes. He was suddenly wearing a fine suit of gold!

Midas pushed open the door. The door turned to gold. He went out to the garden. He touched every rose. Each rose turned to gold.

Now Midas was hungry. He went into the palace. "Bring the King breakfast!" he told his **servants.** "And call for my daughter."

Little Marygold came into the room. She was crying!

"Dear child. What is wrong?" asked the king. "Why are you crying on this fine morning?"

She put out her hand. She was holding a rose from her father's garden.

"It is a beautiful rose," said her father. "It is a rose made of gold!"

"It is *ugly*!" Marygold said. And she cried even louder.

"Dear girl," said the king. "I went into the garden. What did I find? All the beautiful roses have changed. They are all like this one."

She held out her hand. "I do not like roses like this. This rose is hard. And it has no smell. A rose should be soft! And a rose should smell sweet!"

She looked at the rose in her hand. Then she **tossed** it away.

"Do not cry," Midas said. "You can get hundreds of roses for one made of gold."

The servants came in with breakfast for the king. They put the food on the table.

"Let us eat," Midas said.

He picked up some bread. But it turned to gold! Midas stared at the bread. He could not eat gold!

There were rolls on the table. Midas picked up a roll. The roll turned to gold!

Midas reached for an egg. The egg turned to gold! There was water in a glass. He picked up the glass. The glass turned to gold! When the water touched his mouth, the water turned to gold.

The king could not eat. He could not drink. You cannot eat gold! You cannot drink gold!

Marygold jumped out of her chair. She ran to her father's side.

The king put his arms around his child. "Dear girl. Dear girl," King Midas said. He kissed her head. But Marygold had turned to gold! She did not move. She did not speak.

"What have I done!" King Midas said. "What have I done! Dear child! Dear child!"

The king stared sadly at the ground. His eyes were filled with tears.

King Midas heard a sound. He raised his head. He saw the young man standing there.

"Well, King Midas," said the man. "I see you have the Golden Touch. Are you now a happy man?"

"No!" King Midas shook his head. "I am not a happy man. I have never been so sad."

"How can that be?" the young man asked. "You got your wish. Is that not so? You have the Golden Touch. Touch something. It will turn to gold."

"Gold!" King Midas said. "There are more important things than gold! The Golden Touch has cost me Marygold. It has cost me food and drink. How I hate the Golden Touch!"

"Ah!" the young man said. "You are wiser than you were. Do you want to lose the Golden Touch?"

"With all my heart," King Midas said.

"Then hurry to the river," said the man. "Throw yourself into the water. It will wash away your wish. Bring back water from the river. Pour some water on your daughter. You will have her back again."

King Midas did as he was told. He hurried to the river. He threw himself into the water. Suddenly, his heart felt lighter.

Midas stepped out of the water. There were roses growing near the river. Midas touched the roses. The roses did not turn to gold. The Golden Touch was gone!

Midas brought water from the river to his palace. He **poured** the water on his daughter. All at once she came to life! She did not know she had been changed to gold.

Midas went back to the river. He brought back water. Then he went into his garden. He put a drop of water on each rose. Each rose turned red. And each smelled sweet.

Midas smiled. He was a happy man. He never wanted gold again.

The next day Midas went back to the river. He looked at the sand. He saw that the sand was shining brightly. And to this day sand shines like gold.

TELL ABOUT THE STORY.

Put an *x* in the box next to the right answer. Each sentence tells a *fact* about the story.

1. At first King Midas wished that
   - ☐ a. his daughter loved him.
   - ☐ b. he lived in a bigger palace.
   - ☐ c. the roses in his garden were made of gold.

2. The young man gave Midas
   - ☐ a. three wishes.
   - ☐ b. the Golden Touch.
   - ☐ c. bags filled with gold.

3. When Midas put his arms around Marygold, she
   - ☐ a. smiled at him.
   - ☐ b. began to cry.
   - ☐ c. turned to gold.

4. Midas lost the Golden Touch by
   - ☐ a. throwing himself into the river.
   - ☐ b. giving money to the poor.
   - ☐ c. making the young man take it away.

ADD WORDS TO SENTENCES.

Complete the sentences below. Fill in each blank with one of the words in the box. Each word can be found in the story. There are five words and four blanks. This means that one word in the box will not be used.

My Uncle Fred has "the Midas

_____." Whatever he does,
       1

he always _____ money.
                    2

Since everything he touches always

"_____ to gold," Uncle Fred
       3

is "as rich as _____."
                        4

turns	makes
Midas	
touch	smiled

 X 5 =

NUMBER CORRECT   YOUR SCORE

 X 5 =

NUMBER CORRECT   YOUR SCORE

53

LEARN NEW WORDS.

The vocabulary words are printed in **dark type** in the story. You may look back at the words before you answer these questions. Put an *x* in the box next to the right answer.

1. The young man said good-bye and disappeared. When something has *disappeared,* it
   - ☐ a. looks bright.
   - ☐ b. is easy to see.
   - ☐ c. cannot be seen.

2. The king's servants put breakfast on the table. Usually *servants*
   - ☐ a. cook and clean.
   - ☐ b. are soldiers.
   - ☐ c. have a lot of money.

3. Marygold tossed the rose away. The word *tossed* means
   - ☐ a. sold.
   - ☐ b. threw.
   - ☐ c. saved.

4. He poured the water on his daughter. The word *poured* means
   - ☐ a. cleaned.
   - ☐ b. drowned.
   - ☐ c. let fall.

EXPLAIN WHAT HAPPENED.

Here is how to answer these questions. First think about what happened in the story. Then *figure out* (work out) the right answer. This is called *critical thinking.*

1. The story shows that
   - ☐ a. people never change.
   - ☐ b. Marygold did not like roses.
   - ☐ c. some things are more important than gold.

2. When Midas got the Golden Touch, he thought he
   - ☐ a. would always be happy.
   - ☐ b. would not be able to eat.
   - ☐ c. might lose his daughter.

3. Midas put a drop of water on each rose. This shows that he
   - ☐ a. still loved gold.
   - ☐ b. liked real roses more than roses made of gold.
   - ☐ c. was angry with his daughter.

4. When Midas woke up, the chair he touched did not turn to gold. Why?
   - ☐ a. Midas was still very sleepy.
   - ☐ b. The young man had lied.
   - ☐ c. The sun was not yet up.

	× 5 =	
NUMBER CORRECT		YOUR SCORE

	× 5 =	
NUMBER CORRECT		YOUR SCORE

SPOT STORY ELEMENTS.

Some story elements are **plot**, **character**, and **setting**. (See page 3.) Put an *x* in the box next to the right answer.

1. What happened first in the *plot*?
   - ☐ a. Midas saw a young man in the treasure room.
   - ☐ b. Midas jumped into the river.
   - ☐ c. When Midas touched the bread, it turned to gold.

2. Who is the *main character* in the story?
   - ☐ a. King Midas
   - ☐ b. Marygold
   - ☐ c. the young man

3. Which sentence best describes (tells about) the *character* of Midas?
   - ☐ a. He did not love Marygold.
   - ☐ b. At first he loved gold very much.
   - ☐ c. He never liked flowers.

4. The story is *set*
   - ☐ a. a long time ago.
   - ☐ b. a few years ago.
   - ☐ c. today.

☐ × 5 = ☐

NUMBER CORRECT   YOUR SCORE

THINK SOME MORE ABOUT THE STORY.

Your teacher might want you to write your answers.
- Why do you think the young man let Midas lose the Golden Touch?
- Suppose that Midas had not been able to give up the Golden Touch. How you think the story would have ended?
- What lesson or lessons does the story teach?

Write your scores in the boxes below. Then write your score on pages 138 and 139.

☐ **T**ELL ABOUT THE STORY
+
☐ **A**DD WORDS TO SENTENCES
+
☐ **L**EARN NEW WORDS
+
☐ **E**XPLAIN WHAT HAPPENED
+
☐ **S**POT STORY ELEMENTS
=
☐ TOTAL SCORE: Story 4

5

Tea for Two

by Joan Mosby

Before You Read

Before you read "Tea for Two," study the words below. Make sure you know what each word means. This will help you understand the story.

porch: an open place with a roof that is part of a house

calm: not excited; quiet

pale: without much color

force: power. When you use force you try to make someone do something.

boss: someone who runs things or who has power over others

crashed: hit with a loud noise

Tea for Two

by Joan Mosby

Clara and Melissa were sisters. They lived alone. They lived in a big house. It was on the nicest street in town.

One evening their doorbell rang. It was nearly ten o'clock. Melissa was sure of that. She had **glanced** up at the clock on the wall.

Melissa looked at her sister. But Clara shook her head. The two sisters were surprised. The bell almost never rang at that hour. It was much too late. But the bell had rung last night. Now it was ringing again.

"Who could that be?" asked Melissa.

"I do not know," Clara said.

The bell rang again. Clara got up from her chair. She went to the door. Clara was tall and strong. She took long, powerful steps. Her sister, Melissa, was short and thin.

Clara turned on the porch light. Then she opened the door.

"Yes?" she asked.

Suddenly the door was thrown open. It knocked Clara back. A moment later two men were in the house.

One quickly closed the door. The other turned off the porch light.

One of the men looked out the window.

"Do you see anyone?" the other man asked.

"No," said the first. "People don't stay up late in these little towns."

Clara looked at the two men. One was large and heavy. The other was short. He had a very round face.

Clara was sure she had seen them before. But she could not remember where.

"I must ask you to leave!" Clara said. "You must leave at once!"

"We will go in a little while," the large man said. "First we must take care of some business."

"I will call the police!" Clara said. She picked up the phone.

"I would not do that," said the large man. His voice was calm.

The other man came closer. Clara saw that he was holding a gun.

"You better listen to George," said the man with the gun. "Why don't we join your sister?"

Clara put down the phone. Then they all went into the living room.

Melissa was surprised. She looked at the men. "Oh!" she said. "I remember you. You came here last night. You are from the gas company. You said there was a leak. Is there still a problem?"

George smiled. "Yes," he said. "There is still a problem."

"Well! You spent enough time here last night!" Melissa said. "You looked all over this house. You looked from top to bottom. And my sister *told* you there was nothing wrong with the gas!"

Clara said, "Melissa, these men are not from the gas company. They are—I don't know what. Robbers, I guess. They came here last night. But they came to **search** our house."

"I am glad you understand," said George. "Freddy will not point the gun at you. He will keep it in his pocket. But he will have it ready. This is a business call. Do not forget that. Now, please sit down."

Clara sat down next to her sister. George seated himself.

"What do you want here?" Clara asked.

"Money, Miss Weston! Money." said George. "And we are going to get it! We know a lot about this house. We know a lot about you and your sister."

"What do you mean?"

"Your father was Charles Weston. He owned the Weston Lumber Company. He died years ago. You and Melissa got the company. You are the president. That is so, isn't it, Clara?"

Clara did not answer.

George smiled. "The two of you live alone in this house. You have lived here for years. You both have **plenty** of money. But you do not spend very much. You paint the place yourself. You fix things up."

"We know how to take care of ourselves," Clara said.

George laughed, "And you do not believe in banks. You and Melissa do not put your money in banks! You keep it here in the house!"

Clara suddenly turned pale. Melissa's thin hands shook a little.

It was true. Clara did not believe in banks. She had put some money in a bank. That was a long time ago. The bank had gone out of business. Clara got her money back.

But it took a long time. Since then the sisters had never put their money in a bank. People in town knew that.

The large man said, "They call me Gentleman George. People do not get hurt when they do business with me. They just have to listen to me."

"But you are going to rob us!" said Clara.

Gentleman George said, "Please, think of this another way. My friend and I have already done some work here. We had to find out some things. That work took time. We must get paid for our work. We must get paid for our time."

Gentleman George said, "We spent time here last night. That was time well spent. We found out that you have a safe. The safe is in the wall. The safe is behind a painting. It is behind that painting over there."

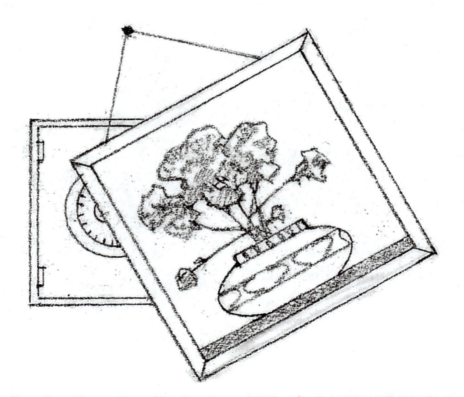

"And you are going to open the safe," Clara said. "Why didn't you do that last night?"

"Ah," said Gentleman George, "Yesterday was Friday. Today is Saturday. We found out that Saturday is the company's busiest day. So today is better. There will be more money in the safe."

"Well," said Clara. "What are you waiting for? Open the safe."

"*I* cannot," said Gentleman George. "*I* do not know the numbers that open the safe. But one of you will open it for me. You both know the right numbers."

"What if we won't?" said Clara.

Gentleman George said, "I believe that you will. We are not in a hurry. I don't want to use force. I don't want to do that. But if we have to . . ."

Clara spoke again. Her voice was hard. She said, "We will *not* open the safe!"

"Maybe not," said Gentleman George.  "Maybe not *we*. But *one* of you will. Melissa might. She might do that to keep us from hurting you."

Gentleman George looked at the gun. It was in Freddy's hand. Melissa began to **sob** softly. Clara put an arm around her sister.

"How very sweet," said Gentleman George. "The strong and the weak. The lion and the lamb."

Clara stared at Gentleman George. There was anger in her eyes.

He said, "You can learn a lot by watching people. I can see that Clara is the boss. Melissa does what Clara says. Clara is strong. Melissa is weak."

Melissa put a handkerchief up to her eyes. Then she looked at the clock.

"Are you expecting someone?" asked Gentleman George.

"No," said Melissa. "But it is ten o'clock. I always make tea at ten o'clock. I do that every night."

Gentleman George said, "Tea every night at ten o'clock. Well, well, well! Each day is just like every other. You work at the office. You put the money in the safe. You have tea at night. Nothing ever changes."

"I suppose it is a little silly," Melissa said softly.

"Oh, no. Not at all," said Gentleman George. "Let us all have tea. That may help you make up your mind about who will open the safe."

Gentleman George got up. He moved to the table. Melissa went to get a teapot.

"Freddy," said Gentleman George. "Go along with Melissa. See that she sticks to making tea. I will stay here with Clara."

Soon Melissa came back. She was carrying a tray. On it was a large, old teapot. There were also four cups.

Melissa put the four cups on the table. She filled Clara's cup with tea. She filled a cup for Gentleman George. Then she filled her own.

Freddy sat down. Melissa began to fill his cup. Suddenly she swung the teapot. It crashed against Freddy's head. Pieces of glass flew into the air. Freddy dropped to the floor.

Gentleman George jumped up from his chair. But he did not take a step. Hot tea from Clara's cup splashed in his face.

He grabbed at his eyes. "I can't see!" he yelled.

When he could open his eyes, he was looking at Freddy's gun. It was in Melissa's hand.

Melissa turned to her sister, "Call the police," she said.

"Whatever you say," Clara answered. "You are the boss."

Clara moved toward the phone. Then she stopped. She said, "It is too bad about the teapot. It broke into a hundred pieces."

Melissa smiled. "Well," she said, "it doesn't matter that much. We only used it for company. You know how we both hate tea!"

TELL ABOUT THE STORY.

Put an *x* in the box next to the right answer. Each sentence tells a *fact* about the story.

1. The men came to the house to
   - ☐ a. have tea with the sisters.
   - ☐ b. fix something that was broken.
   - ☐ c. take money from the safe.

2. Clara and Melissa did not
   - ☐ a. live alone.
   - ☐ b. believe in banks.
   - ☐ c. paint the house themselves.

3. Melissa hit Freddy with
   - ☐ a. the gun.
   - ☐ b. the teapot.
   - ☐ c. a chair.

4. Gentleman George could not see because
   - ☐ a. Clara threw tea in his face.
   - ☐ b. he dropped his glasses.
   - ☐ c. it was dark in the house.

ADD WORDS TO SENTENCES.

Complete the sentences below. Fill in each blank with one of the words in the box. Each word can be found in the story. There are five words and four blanks. This means that one word in the box will not be used.

Every day, _____ all over
                              1
the world drink tea. In England

_____ everyone stops to have
              2
afternoon tea. More _____ is
                                3
used there than in any other place.

Most people buy more than ten

pounds of tea every _____.
                              4

tea	laughed
	year
people	almost

<table>
<tr><td>☐</td><td>X 5 =</td><td>☐</td></tr>
<tr><td>NUMBER CORRECT</td><td></td><td>YOUR SCORE</td></tr>
</table>

<table>
<tr><td>☐</td><td>X 5 =</td><td>☐</td></tr>
<tr><td>NUMBER CORRECT</td><td></td><td>YOUR SCORE</td></tr>
</table>

67

LEARN NEW WORDS.

The vocabulary words are printed in **dark type** in the story. You may look back at the words before you answer these questions. Put an *x* in the box next to the right answer.

1. Melissa glanced at the clock on the wall. The word *glanced* means
   - ☐ a. fixed.
   - ☐ b. looked.
   - ☐ c. bought.

2. The men came to search the house. The word *search* means
   - ☐ a. to talk about.
   - ☐ b. to look through.
   - ☐ c. to break into pieces.

3. Clara and Melissa had plenty of money. The word *plenty* means
   - ☐ a. a lot of.
   - ☐ b. some.
   - ☐ c. none.

4. Melissa began to sob, so Clara put an arm around her sister. The word *sob* means to
   - ☐ a. fight.
   - ☐ b. shout.
   - ☐ c. cry.

EXPLAIN WHAT HAPPENED.

Here is how to answer these questions. First think about what happened in the story. Then *figure out* (work out) the right answer. This is called *critical thinking*.

1. We may infer (figure out) that
   - ☐ a. the sisters were poor.
   - ☐ b. George got away.
   - ☐ c. nothing was wrong with the gas.

2. Which sentence is true?
   - ☐ a. Clara did not know how to open the safe.
   - ☐ b. The sisters liked tea.
   - ☐ c. The sisters did not drink tea every night.

3. George said that Clara and Melissa were "the lion and the lamb." He was saying that
   - ☐ a. both sisters were weak.
   - ☐ b. Clara was strong and Melissa was weak.
   - ☐ c. they did not like him.

4. It is fair to say that the sisters
   - ☐ a. tricked the men.
   - ☐ b. were too scared to think.
   - ☐ c. had no money in the safe.

☐ X 5 = ☐
NUMBER CORRECT | YOUR SCORE

☐ X 5 = ☐
NUMBER CORRECT | YOUR SCORE

SPOT STORY ELEMENTS.
Some story elements are **plot**, **character**, and **setting**. (See page 3.) Put an *x* in the box next to the right answer.

1. What happened first in the *plot*?
   - ☐ a. Melissa told Clara to call the police.
   - ☐ b. Two men pushed open the door.
   - ☐ c. Melissa came into the room with a teapot and cups.

2. Which sentence best *characterizes* (tells about) Clara?
   - ☐ a. She was tall and looked strong.
   - ☐ b. She was short and thin.
   - ☐ c. She was small and had a very round face.

3. Where is the story *set*?
   - ☐ a. in a store
   - ☐ b. in an office
   - ☐ c. in a big house

4. When is the story *set*?
   - ☐ a. in the morning
   - ☐ b. around noon
   - ☐ c. about ten o'clock at night

☐	× 5 = ☐
NUMBER CORRECT	YOUR SCORE

THINK SOME MORE ABOUT THE STORY.
Your teacher might want you to write your answers.

- Gentleman George said that Clara was the boss. Why did he believe that? Was he right? Explain.
- Do you think that Melissa really was crying—or was she pretending? Explain.
- Clara told the men, "We know how to take care of ourselves." Show how that was true.

Write your scores in the boxes below. Then write your scores on pages 138 and 139.

☐
+
TELL ABOUT THE STORY

☐
+
ADD WORDS TO SENTENCES

☐
+
LEARN NEW WORDS

☐
+
EXPLAIN WHAT HAPPENED

☐
=
SPOT STORY ELEMENTS

☐
TOTAL SCORE: Story 5

6
Anansi and the Sea

A West African folktale

Before You Read

Before you read "Anansi and the Sea," study the words below. Make sure you know what each word means. This will help you understand the story.

crops: plants used for food

hut: a small house

island: land that has water all around it

appeared: could be seen

melted: changed by heat into a liquid (something that flows like water). When ice becomes warm, it melts.

punish: to make someone suffer for doing something wrong

Anansi and the Sea

a West African folktale

Have you read about Anansi? There are many stories about him. The stories take place in West Africa. Anansi is very clever. He is also very **selfish**. He often tries to trick people. But he does not get away with his tricks.

Many of the stories about Anansi are funny. Some are sad. Most of the stories teach a lesson. This is one of them.

Anansi lived in a small village with his wife and children. It had not rained for many months. The crops had died. There was not enough food for the people. The people of the village were hungry.

73

One day Anansi was sitting outside his hut. He was looking out toward the sea. He was thinking, "I am very hungry. I wish I had something to eat. I have not had a good meal in a long time."

Suddenly, Anansi saw something in the middle of the sea. It was a tiny island. Anansi looked closer. He saw a tall tree growing on the island.

Anansi said to himself, "That island is far away. If only I could get there. I would climb that tree. I might find fruit on the tree."

Anansi walked down to the sea. He looked around. He saw an old boat lying on its side. The boat was small. It did not look very strong. But Anansi pulled the boat into the water. He got in the boat and began to row.

The waves were very strong. They pushed the boat back. Six times Anansi tried to get to the island. Six times the waves pushed him back. Anansi said, "I will try one more time."

This time the boat went over the waves. Anansi rowed as hard as he could. He rowed and rowed. It took a long time. But he finally got to the island.

Anansi tied the boat to the tree. He looked up at the tree. There was fruit at the top.

Anansi began to climb the tree. He got to the top. Then he picked a piece of fruit off the tree. He dropped the fruit down to the boat. But the fruit missed the boat. It fell into the water.

Anansi picked another piece of fruit. He looked down at the boat. He dropped the fruit. Again it missed the boat. The fruit fell into the sea.

"Aighhh!" cried Anansi. He threw up his arms. Suddenly, Anansi was falling. *SPLASH!* He hit the water. He went down, down, down, down.

"I will drown!" Anansi thought to himself. He kept going down.

To his surprise, Anansi did not drown. He found himself standing at the bottom of the sea. He looked around. He saw a pretty little **cottage.** An old man came out of the cottage. The man looked at Anansi.

The man said, "I am the King of the Sea. What do you want? You must want something very much. Yes. You must want it very much to come down here to my cottage."

Anansi said, "I am hungry. I want food very much."

Anansi told his story to the King of the Sea. Anansi said, "It has not rained in my land. All the crops have died. Everyone is very hungry."

"I see," said the King of the Sea. "Your people have no food. That is sad. Very sad."

The King of the Sea went into his cottage. He came out with a large pot. He gave the pot to Anansi.

"Take this pot," said the King of the Sea. "It will make food for you and your family. You will never be hungry again."

Anansi was very happy. He thanked the old man. He took the pot and left the bottom of the sea.

Anansi could not wait to try out the pot. He hurried back to the boat. He sat down. Then he said, "Pot. Pot. What you did for your master, do now for me."

At once all kinds of good food appeared. Anansi ate the food. It was a wonderful meal. It was the best meal that he ever had.

Then Anansi began to row. He felt better now. He rowed very fast. Before long Anansi reached land.

Anansi said to himself, "I will run home. I will show my family this pot. They will have a good meal.

They will enjoy it very much."

Anansi was almost home. Then he thought to himself, "My family may use up all the food the pot makes. Then there will be nothing left for me. I better not tell them about the pot. That way, I can have a good meal when I want one."

Anansi got to his house. There was no one home. He went to his room. He **hid** the pot. Then he lay down on his bed. He made believe he was hungry and tired.

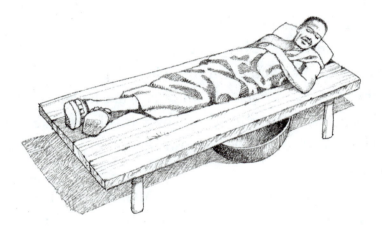

Later his wife and children came home. "Where have you been?" asked Anansi's wife.

"I have been looking for food," Anansi said. "I could not find any."

"There is no food to be found," said Mrs. Anansi.

"That is so," said Anansi. "There is no food."

Anansi's wife and children were hungry. But Anansi did not think about them. All he cared about was the wonderful pot in his room.

When Anansi was hungry, he went to his room. There he had a good meal. Anansi's family got thinner and thinner. But Anansi got fatter and fatter.

"This is very strange," thought Mrs. Anansi. "My husband is getting fat. But we are growing thinner."

One afternoon Anansi was hungry. He went to his room and closed the door. He spoke to the pot. The pot filled with food. Anansi had a fine meal. Then he put away the pot.

Anansi's son, Kweku, was standing outside the window. Kweku saw what happened.

Kweku waited until his father left the house. Then Kweku went to his father's room. He found the pot. He brought it to his mother. He told her what he had seen.

Mrs. Anansi called the other children. They spoke to the pot. The pot filled with food. And the hungry family had a wonderful meal.

When they finished eating, Mrs. Anansi said, "It was wrong for your father to hide this pot. I will take it to the village. Everyone in the village will have a good meal."

Mrs. Anansi took the pot into the village. She called the villagers together. The pot began to make food. People heard about the pot. More and more villagers came. The pot made more and more food. It got hotter and hotter and hotter. And then suddenly—it was gone! The pot had melted away!

What could be done? Anansi would be very angry.

Mrs. Anansi told her children, "Do not say a word about the pot."

Anansi came home later. He was hungry and wanted his supper. He went into his room. He went to the hiding place. He looked for the pot. But the pot was gone!

Anansi was very angry. Where was the pot? Someone must have found it! It must be someone in his family! He would find out who it was. He would punish that person! But first he had something to do.

Anansi said nothing. He waited until morning. Then he went down to the sea. He found the old boat. He pulled it into the water. He got into the boat and began to row.

This time the boat moved very **swiftly**. It went over the waves. It went straight to the little island.

Anansi wanted to see the King of the Sea. So Anansi did the same thing he did before. He tied the boat to the tree. He climbed to the top of the tree. He picked a piece of fruit. He dropped the fruit down to the boat. But this time the fruit did not miss! It went straight into the boat.

Anansi picked more pieces of fruit. He dropped them down. They went into the boat. Anansi was surprised.

He looked down at the water. Then Anansi jumped. *SPLASH!* He went down, down, down, down. Soon he was standing at the bottom of the sea. Anansi looked around. He saw the little cottage.

Anansi knocked on the door. "Who is there?" called the King of the Sea.

"It is me—Anansi."

The King of the Sea opened the door. "How can I help you?" he asked.

Anansi told the old man the whole story. Anansi finished by saying, "So I hid the pot. And now someone has taken it."

"I see," said the King of the Sea. He shook his head. Then he said, "I have something to give you."

This time he gave Anansi a very fine stick.

"Good-bye," said the King of the Sea.

Anansi hurried back to the boat. He could not wait to try his new gift.

"Stick, stick," Anansi said. "What you did for your master, do now for me."

The stick began to beat Anansi. It would not stop. It beat him on his arms and legs. It beat his back.

Finally, Anansi stood up. He jumped out of the boat. He landed in the water. He began to swim.

After a while Anansi reached land. He looked back at the sea. The boat was gone. And he could no longer see the little island.

Slowly Anansi walked back to his house. His arms and legs hurt. His back hurt too. Anansi was sad. He knew he should have acted more wisely right from the start.

TELL ABOUT THE STORY.

Put an *x* in the box next to the right answer. Each sentence tells a *fact* about the story.

1. The people in Anansi's village were
   - ☐ a. hungry.
   - ☐ b. happy.
   - ☐ c. young.

2. Anansi climbed a tree to get
   - ☐ a. leaves.
   - ☐ b. fruit.
   - ☐ c. wood.

3. Mrs. Anansi gave food to
   - ☐ a. Anansi and his friends.
   - ☐ b. the King of the Sea.
   - ☐ c. the people of the village.

4. At the end of the story, the King of the Sea gave Anansi
   - ☐ a. money.
   - ☐ b. food.
   - ☐ c. a stick.

ADD WORDS TO SENTENCES.

Complete the sentences below. Fill in each blank with one of the words in the box. Each word can be found in the story. There are five words and four blanks. This means that one word in the box will not be used.

Every day, rain _____

somewhere on the earth. It is true

that _____ is important for

life. If there is too little rain, trees

and plants die and there is not

_____ food. But too much

rain can also _____ crops.

drown	enough
	rain
hungry	falls

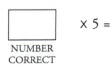

☐ X 5 = ☐
NUMBER   YOUR
CORRECT   SCORE

☐ X 5 = ☐
NUMBER   YOUR
CORRECT   SCORE

LEARN NEW WORDS.

The vocabulary words are printed in **dark type** in the story. You may look back at the words before you answer these questions. Put an *x* in the box next to the right answer.

1. Anansi was selfish and kept the pot. Someone who is *selfish*
   - [ ] a. always helps others.
   - [ ] b. cares too little about others.
   - [ ] c. has many friends.

2. An old man lived in the cottage. The word *cottage* means
   - [ ] a. a small house.
   - [ ] b. a tall tree.
   - [ ] c. some large rocks.

3. Anansi hid the pot. The word *hid* means
   - [ ] a. lost.
   - [ ] b. told about.
   - [ ] c. put in a place that is hard to find.

4. The boat moved swiftly and soon reached land. The word *swiftly* means
   - [ ] a. quickly.
   - [ ] b. slowly.
   - [ ] c. loudly.

EXPLAIN WHAT HAPPENED.

Here is how to answer these questions. First think about what happened in the story. Then *figure out* (work out) the right answer. This is called *critical thinking*.

1. The King of the Sea probably gave the pot to Anansi because the old man
   - [ ] a. did not like the pot.
   - [ ] b. felt sorry for Anansi and the others.
   - [ ] c. did not need the pot.

2. Anansi wanted to make sure that
   - [ ] a. his wife had enough food.
   - [ ] b. everyone had enough food.
   - [ ] c. he had enough food.

3. Anansi's family was probably surprised that he
   - [ ] a. kept getting fatter.
   - [ ] b. looked for food.
   - [ ] c. could row so well.

4. The last line of the story shows that Anansi
   - [ ] a. was no longer hungry.
   - [ ] b. knew he did the wrong thing.
   - [ ] c. would never change.

<table>
<tr><td></td><td>X 5 =</td><td></td></tr>
<tr><td>NUMBER CORRECT</td><td></td><td>YOUR SCORE</td></tr>
</table>

<table>
<tr><td></td><td>X 5 =</td><td></td></tr>
<tr><td>NUMBER CORRECT</td><td></td><td>YOUR SCORE</td></tr>
</table>

SPOT STORY ELEMENTS.

Some story elements are **plot**, **character**, and **setting**. (See page 3.) Put an *x* in the box next to the right answer.

1. What happened last in the *plot*?
   - ☐ a. The stick began to beat Anansi.
   - ☐ b. Anansi saw a tree on the island.
   - ☐ c. The old man gave Anansi a pot.

2. The *main character* in the story is
   - ☐ a. the King of the Sea.
   - ☐ b. Mrs. Anansi.
   - ☐ c. Anansi.

3. Which sentence best describes (tells about) the *character* of Anansi?
   - ☐ a. He cared very much about his family.
   - ☐ b. He liked to help others.
   - ☐ c. He tried to trick others.

4. The story is *set* in
   - ☐ a. West Africa.
   - ☐ b. Florida.
   - ☐ c. New York.

☐ NUMBER CORRECT x 5 = ☐ YOUR SCORE

THINK SOME MORE ABOUT THE STORY.

Your teacher might want you to write your answers.

- Why do you think the King of the Sea gave Anansi the stick? Do you think that was the right thing for the King of the Sea to do? Explain.
- Suppose that Anansi had told his family about the pot. How do you think the story would have ended?
- What lesson or lessons does the story teach?

Write your scores in the boxes below. Then write your score on pages 138 and 139.

☐ **T**ELL ABOUT THE STORY

\+

☐ **A**DD WORDS TO SENTENCES

\+

☐ **L**EARN NEW WORDS

\+

☐ **E**XPLAIN WHAT HAPPENED

\+

☐ **S**POT STORY ELEMENTS

\=

☐ TOTAL SCORE: Story 6

7
Clever Grethel

an old tale

Before You Read

Before you read "Clever Grethel," study the words below.
Make sure you know what each word means. This will
help you understand the story.

clever: bright; smart

roast: to cook or bake meat

serve: to put out food and drink

arrived: came to a place

inn: a place where people can stop to eat and to sleep

sharpen: to make sharp; to give a thin cutting edge

Clever Grethel

an old tale

There once was a cook. Her name was Grethel. She was so clever that everyone called her Clever Grethel.

Clever Grethel was a very fine cook. She made turkey pie. She made pumpkin soup. She made apple cake.

There was nothing that she could not make. And everything she made was very, very good.

Clever Grethel worked for Mr. James. One day Mr. James said to Clever Grethel, "I have **invited** a friend to dinner tonight. I know what he likes. Can you roast two chickens for us?"

"I can and I will," said Clever Grethel.

"Will you make sure the birds are fat and sweet?"

"I can and I will," said Clever Grethel.

"And can you serve the meal at six o'clock?"

"I can and I will," said Clever Grethel.

Clever Grethel went to the store. She found two fine chickens. They were large and fat. She paid for the birds. Then she took them home.

Clever Grethel cleaned the birds. She **stuffed** them with fruits and nuts and pieces of bread. She put them on the fire. After a while they began to get brown.

Before long it was nearly six o'clock. But Mr. James's friend had not arrived.

Clever Grethel said to Mr. James, "Your friend is late. He is not here. I must take the birds off the fire soon. If I do not, they will surely burn."

Mr. James went to the window. He looked outside. "I do not see my friend," he said.

Clever Grethel shook her head. She said, "The birds are almost ready now."

Mr. James said, "My friend may be coming up the path. I will go outside to see." He went to look.

Clever Grethel took the chickens off the fire. "My," she thought. "Don't these birds look good! They look good enough to eat!"

Clever Grethel sat down on a chair. She waited and waited and waited some more. Then she thought to herself, "These poor birds are getting cold." She rubbed some butter on the birds. Then she put them back on the fire again. Soon they smelled so good that her mouth began to water.

She said, "These chickens should be eaten *now*! Someone should eat them. Someone really should!"

She looked around. Of course, no one was there.

Clever Grethel ran to the door. She looked outside. She did not see Mr. James. She did not see his friend.

Clever Grethel went back to the kitchen. "Oh, dear!" she exclaimed, "This bird's wing is beginning to burn."

She cut off the wing with her kitchen knife. Then she thought, "I better eat this wing. I will eat it now. That will get it out of the way."

So she ate the wing. It tasted very good.

Clever Grethel looked at the bird again. "Dear me," she sighed, "how strange this chicken looks. It has one wing off. It has one wing on. Did you ever see such a funny thing? I better cut off the other wing." So she cut the wing off. Then she ate it up.

Clever Grethel went to the door again. She looked outside.

"Well," she said, "I still do not see Mr. James or his friend. I do not see them anywhere. It is getting late. Perhaps they stopped at an inn. Perhaps they are eating dinner there. I wonder if they are coming back. Who knows? Not me."

She looked at the birds. "Dear me," she said. "Once these two chickens looked the same. It was not possible to tell them apart. But look at them now! One has *two* wings. The other has *none*. That is not right! That is not fair! What is good for one is good for the other!"

So she cut the wings off the *other* bird. Then she quickly ate them up.

She looked at the chickens. They had no wings. Clever Grethel began to worry. Then she said to herself, "There is nothing for me to worry about. It is very late. It is too late for Mr. James's friend to have dinner here. I might as well finish eating his chicken."

That did not take Clever Grethel very long. She ate the bird. She ate it all up. She ate the skin. She ate the meat. She ate the fruits and nuts and pieces of bread. All that was left was a little hill of bones.

"Ah, well, Grethel," she said to herself. "You are a very good cook. That was a very fine meal. It surely was!"

Clever Grethel looked at the other bird. It seemed so lonely by itself. It did not even have its wings! She said, "What is fair is fair! What is good for one is good for the other!" And so she began to eat the second bird.

She ate half that chicken. Then Mr. James ran in.

"Hurry!" he called. "Hurry! Serve the food! My friend will be here in a minute or two. I see him walking up the path."

Mr. James did not stop to look around. He grabbed a large kitchen knife to **carve** the birds. He grabbed a little knife to sharpen the big one.

Mr. James rushed out. As he did, he yelled, "Hurry! Hurry! Bring out the dinner!"

"I can and I will," answered Clever Grethel. But she did not move. She just stood there. She thought about what to do.

Mr. James's friend knocked softly on the front door. Clever Grethel hurried to the door. She opened it. She stepped outside. She put a finger to her lips.

"Ssshhhhh!" she told Mr. James's friend. "Do not say a word! You must listen to me. You must save yourself! Mr. James is wild with anger because you are late. The poor man has gone out of his mind. He is mad! He is *mad*! He has two knives. And he is waiting for you. He said he was going to cut off both of your ears!"

The friend turned pale. He did not move. Then he heard a sound. It came from inside the house. It was the sound of knives being sharpened against each other.

The friend turned. He ran. He ran as fast as he could go.

Clever Grethel closed the door. She went inside. "Well, Mr. James!" she cried. "That was a fine friend you invited to dinner tonight!"

"Why? What do you mean?" asked Mr. James. He was still holding the knives in his hand.

"What do I mean?" said Clever Grethel. "Just listen to this! Your friend knocked on the door. I opened it. He stepped inside. He put his nose up in the air. 'Is that roast chicken I smell?' said he. He did not say another word. He **dashed** into the kitchen. He grabbed the two beautiful birds that I had there. Then he ran off down the street with them!"

"Ran off down the street with them!" said Mr., James. "Ran off down the street with *both* of the birds!"

"Ran off down the street with *both* of the birds!" said Clever Grethel.

"He might have left me *one* for dinner," said Mr. James. "I only want one! I only want *one*!"

Mr. James rushed out of the house. He started running after his friend. As he ran, Mr. James called out, "Stop! I only want one! I only want one!"

The friend looked back. He saw Mr. James running after him. He saw that Mr. James had two knives in his hands. Mr. James was calling, "I only want one!"

The friend thought to himself, "He wants one of my ears! He only wants *one*!"

This made the friend run even faster.

At the house Clever Grethel went into the kitchen. There was still half a chicken there. She looked at it. Then she said, "I must finish eating this bird. I must eat it all before Mr. James comes back. I can and I will."

And Clever Grethel did!

TELL ABOUT THE STORY.

Put an *x* in the box next to the right answer. Each sentence tells a *fact* about the story.

1. Mr. James asked Clever Grethel to make sure the chickens were
   - ☐ a. fat and sweet.
   - ☐ b. very small.
   - ☐ c. ready at five o'clock

2. Mr. James's friend came to the house
   - ☐ a. on time.
   - ☐ b. a few minutes late.
   - ☐ c. very late.

3. Grethel told the friend that Mr. James was
   - ☐ a. too tired to see him.
   - ☐ b. glad he was there.
   - ☐ c. wild with anger.

4. The friend thought that Mr. James wanted
   - ☐ a. one of his chickens.
   - ☐ b. one of his ears.
   - ☐ c. him to come back to the house for dinner.

ADD WORDS TO SENTENCES.

Complete the sentences below. Fill in each blank with one of the words in the box. Each word can be found in the story. There are five words and four blanks. This means that one word in the box will not be used.

The kitchen may be the most important room in the _____.
1

Some families spend more time together in the _____ than in
2

any other room. It is often the place where the family _____. And
3

many people use the kitchen table as a desk for _____.
4

kitchen	work
eats	
finish	house

☐ X 5 = ☐

NUMBER CORRECT   YOUR SCORE

☐ X 5 = ☐

NUMBER CORRECT   YOUR SCORE

LEARN NEW WORDS.

The vocabulary words are printed in **dark type** in the story. You may look back at the words before you answer these questions. Put an *x* in the box next to the right answer.

1. Mr. James invited a friend to dinner. The word *invited* means
   - ☐ a. asked.
   - ☐ b. sent.
   - ☐ c. forgot.

2. She stuffed the birds with fruit and nuts. The word *stuffed* means
   - ☐ a. bought.
   - ☐ b. killed.
   - ☐ c. filled.

3. He grabbed a kitchen knife to carve the birds. The word *carve* means
   - ☐ a. fight.
   - ☐ b. cut.
   - ☐ c. push.

4. Grethel said that he dashed into the kitchen and took the birds. The word *dashed* means
   - ☐ a. ran quickly.
   - ☐ b. stayed away.
   - ☐ c. looked up.

☐ X 5 =	☐
NUMBER CORRECT	YOUR SCORE

EXPLAIN WHAT HAPPENED.

Here is how to answer these questions. First think about what happened in the story. Then *figure out* (work out) the right answer. This is called *critical thinking*.

1. Clever Grethel ate the birds because
   - ☐ a. they were hers.
   - ☐ b. she knew that Mr. James would not come back.
   - ☐ c. they made her very hungry.

2. Clever Grethel probably did not
   - ☐ a. enjoy eating the chickens.
   - ☐ b. know how to cook well.
   - ☐ c. plan to eat both birds.

3. Which sentence is true?
   - ☐ a. The friend ran away with the birds.
   - ☐ b. Mr. James and his friend believed Clever Grethel.
   - ☐ c. Grethel left one of the chickens for Mr. James.

4. The story shows that Clever Grethel was good at
   - ☐ a. making up stories.
   - ☐ b. writing stories.
   - ☐ c. running fast.

☐ X 5 =	☐
NUMBER CORRECT	YOUR SCORE

SPOT STORY ELEMENTS.

Some story elements are **plot**, **character**, and **setting**. (See page 3.) Put an *x* in the box next to the right answer.

1. What happened first in the *plot*?
   - ☐ a. Grethel cut off a wing.
   - ☐ b. Grethel bought chickens.
   - ☐ c. Mr. James ran after his friend.

2. Who is the *main character* in the story?
   - ☐ a. Mr. James
   - ☐ b. Clever Grethel
   - ☐ c. the friend

3. Which sentence best describes (tells about) the *character* of Clever Grethel?
   - ☐ a. She was a good cook who was very clever.
   - ☐ b. Although she was a good cook, she was not clever.
   - ☐ c. She was not clever.

4. The story is *set*
   - ☐ a. in a store.
   - ☐ b. at an inn.
   - ☐ c. in and around Mr. James's house.

☐ × 5 = ☐

NUMBER CORRECT   YOUR SCORE

THINK SOME MORE ABOUT THE STORY.

Your teacher might want you to write your answers.
- How did Clever Grethel get her name? Was it a good name for her? Why?
- Explain why the friend believed Clever Grethel's story.
- Why did Grethel have to finish eating the chicken before Mr. James came home?

Write your scores in the boxes below. Then write your scores on pages 138 and 139.

☐ **T**ELL ABOUT THE STORY
\+
☐ **A**DD WORDS TO SENTENCES
\+
☐ **L**EARN NEW WORDS
\+
☐ **E**XPLAIN WHAT HAPPENED
\+
☐ **S**POT STORY ELEMENTS
=
☐ TOTAL SCORE: Story 7

8
Fresh Fish Sold Here

by Angel Flores

Before You Read

Before you read "Fresh Fish Sold Here," study the words below. Make sure you know what each word means. This will help you understand the story.

pesos: money used in some countries

decided: made up one's mind. When you decide, you choose to do something.

fresh: new. Fresh fish are fish that have just been caught.

remove: take away

perfume: something that smells very sweet

Fresh Fish
Sold Here

by Angel Flores

Pedro was a fisherman. He loved his work. In the morning he went out in a boat. He fished until dark. Then he rowed back.

Pedro sold the fish he had caught. He sold them to the villagers. They came down to the **shore.** They waited there for the fishermen.

Pedro was a very good fisherman. He always caught many fish. But he did not make much money. Still, he made enough to live on. And he was able to save some pesos.

Pedro was happy. He never **complained.** He liked to fish. He liked the fresh air. And he liked the sea.

Pedro had a friend named Carlos. One day Carlos and Pedro were talking. Carlos said, "Pedro, you should open a store. You should sell fish. You know many fishermen. They will sell you their fish. You can sell a lot of fish in a store. You will make a lot of money. You will make more money than you are making now."

Pedro thought about this. He liked the idea. But he was worried. He said, "I never sold fish in a store."

Carlos said, "Do not worry. It is easy. Don't you sell fish now? You can sell fish in a store. Everyone in the village likes you. People know you are **honest.** They will buy fish from you."

"Do you think so?" asked Pedro.

"Oh, yes," said Carlos. "Your store will do well." Carlos thought for a moment. Then he said, "The most important thing is the sign."

"The sign?" Pedro asked.

"The sign," Carlos said. "First you must put up a big sign. It must be a good sign. People will read the sign. Then they will come into your store."

"Are you sure?" asked Pedro.

"Of course I am sure," said Carlos. "Think about the sign. The sign is very important."

Pedro decided to open a store. He remembered what Carlos had said. He thought about the sign. He thought for a long time. He needed a good sign.

Finally, he knew what the sign should say. Pedro called a sign painter. Pedro told the painter what to write on the sign. The sign cost a lot of money. It was very large. The words were very big. They were painted in bright colors. This is what the sign said:

FRESH FISH SOLD HERE

Pedro was very happy with the sign.

The first **customer** came into the store. She bought some fish. Then she said to Pedro, "Why do you have the word HERE on the sign? Everyone knows that it is *here* where fish are sold. The store is *here*. It is not on another block. You do not need the word HERE on your sign."

Pedro thought about what the lady said. "She is right," Pedro told himself. "I do not need the word HERE."

Pedro called the painter. Pedro said, "Please remove the word HERE from my sign."

The painter came to the store. He took the word HERE off the sign.

The next morning a man came to Pedro's store. The man bought some fish. The man was just about to leave. Then he turned around. He said, "Pedro, there is something wrong with your sign."

"Wrong?" said Pedro. "Wrong? What is wrong with my sign?"

The man said, "You do not need the word SOLD on your sign. Everyone knows that fish are *sold* in the store. Nobody thinks that the fish are free. No one thinks that you *give* them away."

Pedro thought about this. "Yes, that is so," Pedro told the man.

The man said, "Your sign will be better without the word SOLD. The only words that you need are FRESH FISH."

"You are right," Pedro said. So Pedro called the painter again. The painter came to the store. He removed the word SOLD from the sign.

Two days later a man from the telephone company came to Pedro's store. The man bought some fish. Then the man said, "I like your sign. I like it very much. It is a beautiful sign."

Pedro smiled. His heart was filled with joy.

The man said, "But there is one thing the matter with your sign."

"The matter with my sign?" said Pedro. "What is the matter with my sign?"

The man said, "You do not need the word FRESH on your sign. Everyone knows that you cannot sell fish that are *old.* Everyone knows that fish *must* be fresh. You do not need the word FRESH on your sign. Your sign should say FISH. FISH is enough."

"I see what you mean," Pedro told the man. "I will have the word FRESH removed from the sign."

The painter came that day. He took the word FRESH off the sign.

105

Pedro looked at his sign. It said FISH. Pedro thought to himself, "It cost a lot to keep changing the sign. But now it is right." Pedro felt good.

Two days later a fisherman passed by Pedro's store. The fisherman stood on the other side of the street. "Pedro!" the fisherman called. "What a fool you are! From far away, everyone can tell that *fish* are sold there. Why do you need that sign? You do not need the word FISH. Everyone can tell you sell *fish*. Fish smell like *fish*. They do not smell like perfume!"

So Pedro had the last word removed.

The next morning Carlos came by. Carlos was surprised. "Pedro!" said Carlos. "Don't you remember what I said? You must have a sign! The most important thing is the sign!"

Pedro did not say a word. He walked out of his store. He went down to the water. He got into his boat. He began to fish. And he has been a happy man ever since.

TELL ABOUT THE STORY.

Put an *x* in the box next to the right answer. Each sentence tells a *fact* about the story.

1. Carlos thought that Pedro should
   ☐ a. open a store.
   ☐ b. become a painter.
   ☐ c. give Carlos a job.

2. Pedro's sign was very
   ☐ a. small.
   ☐ b. large.
   ☐ c. old.

3. Pedro kept calling the painter to ask him to
   ☐ a. buy fish.
   ☐ b. take a word off the sign.
   ☐ c. put some more words on the sign.

4. When Carlos did not see a sign, he was
   ☐ a. angry.
   ☐ b. happy.
   ☐ c. surprised.

ADD WORDS TO SENTENCES.

Complete the sentences below. Fill in each blank with one of the words in the box. Each word can be found in the story. There are five words and four blanks. This means that one word in the box will not be used.

Did you _____ there are
        1

more than forty thousand different

kinds of fish? They live in bodies of

_____ all around the world.
      2

There are far _____ fish than
                3

any other animal on earth. There are

more _____ than *all* the other
            4

animals together!

water	idea
know	
fish	more

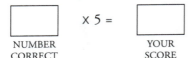

NUMBER CORRECT   x 5 =   YOUR SCORE

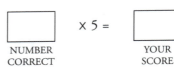

NUMBER CORRECT   x 5 =   YOUR SCORE

107

LEARN NEW WORDS.

The vocabulary words are printed in **dark type** in the story. You may look back at the words before you answer these questions. Put an *x* in the box next to the right answer.

1. The villagers came down to the shore. The word *shore* means
   - ☐ a. a large boat.
   - ☐ b. the middle of the sea.
   - ☐ c. the land at the edge of the water.

2. Pedro was happy and never complained. The word *complained* means
   - ☐ a. said something was wrong.
   - ☐ b. told funny stories.
   - ☐ c. had many friends.

3. People liked Pedro because he was honest. Someone who is *honest*
   - ☐ a. is poor.
   - ☐ b. is fair and does not lie.
   - ☐ c. is always happy.

4. A customer came into Pedro's store. A *customer* is someone who
   - ☐ a. sells things.
   - ☐ b. works hard.
   - ☐ c. buys or shops.

EXPLAIN WHAT HAPPENED.

Here is how to answer these questions. First think about what happened in the story. Then *figure out* (work out) the right answer. This is called *critical thinking*.

1. People probably went to Pedro's store because
   - ☐ a. he gave away fish.
   - ☐ b. they knew him and liked him.
   - ☐ c. no other store was near.

2. The story shows that Pedro
   - ☐ a. had no money.
   - ☐ b. never listened to anyone.
   - ☐ c. usually listened to what people said.

3. Pedro wanted his sign to be
   - ☐ a. bigger than any other sign.
   - ☐ b. small but beautiful.
   - ☐ c. just right.

4. Which sentence is true?
   - ☐ a. Being happy was more important than money to Pedro.
   - ☐ b. Money was the most important thing to Pedro.
   - ☐ c. Pedro had no friends.

☐ × 5 = ☐	
NUMBER CORRECT YOUR SCORE	

☐ × 5 = ☐	
NUMBER CORRECT YOUR SCORE	

108

SPOT STORY ELEMENTS.

Some story elements are **plot**, **character**, and **setting**. (See page 3.) Put an *x* in the box next to the right answer.

1. What happened first in the *plot*?
   - ☐ a. A fisherman called Pedro a fool.
   - ☐ b. The painter took the word HERE off the sign.
   - ☐ c. Pedro opened a store.

2. Who is the *main character* in the story?
   - ☐ a. Pedro
   - ☐ b. Carlos
   - ☐ c. a man from the telephone company

3. Which sentence best *characterizes* (tells about) Pedro?
   - ☐ a. He was a very good fisherman who loved to fish.
   - ☐ b. He liked working in a store.
   - ☐ c. He made a lot of money.

4. Where is the story *set*?
   - ☐ a. in a city
   - ☐ b. in a village
   - ☐ c. in a large, busy town

☐ × 5 = ☐

NUMBER CORRECT   YOUR SCORE

THINK SOME MORE ABOUT THE STORY.

Your teacher might want you to write your answers.

- At the end of the story, Pedro gave up his store and went back to fishing. Do you think he did the right thing? Why?
- Should Pedro have listened to any of the people who told him to change his sign? If so, which person? Explain your answer.
- Why do you think Pedro did not tell Carlos about what happened to the sign?

Write your scores in the boxes below. Then write your scores on pages 138 and 139.

☐ **T**ELL ABOUT THE STORY
+
☐ **A**DD WORDS TO SENTENCES
+
☐ **L**EARN NEW WORDS
+
☐ **E**XPLAIN WHAT HAPPENED
+
☐ **S**POT STORY ELEMENTS
=
☐ TOTAL SCORE: Story 8

9
The Fire

by Shirley Nagel

Before You Read

Before you read "The Fire," study the words below. Make sure you know what each word means. This will help you understand the story.

center: the middle

understood: got the meaning of

breathe: to take air into the lungs and let it out

blanket: a soft, heavy cover used to keep people warm

ducked: moved the head down

The Fire

by Shirley Nagel

Mary turned over in her sleeping bag. It was late at night. It was so quiet in the country. Even the birds were asleep.

Mary was dreaming. She was dreaming about her grandfather. They called him the Old One. She dreamed about him often ever since he died.

In this dream he was calling to her. She could hear his voice. And she saw him. He was pointing to something.

The Old One's voice seemed far away. But he was calling her name. It was not the name she used in the city. It was her Indian name.

Her Indian name was Eyes-Looking-Up. Her parents gave her that name when she was a baby. They said she was always looking up. She was always watching the sky.

That was so. During the day she looked up at the clouds. At night she looked at the stars for hours. So they called her Eyes-Looking-Up.

Eyes-Looking-Up was Mary's name until she was six. Then her father moved the family away. They moved away from the reservation. There was no school near the Indian reservation. The nearest one was many miles away. Her father wanted the family to live closer to a school. So they moved to the city.

That was eleven years ago. Now Eyes-Looking-Up
was seventeen. She had a job. She was a counselor. She
worked in a summer camp. She took care of young
children. And she had a new name. It was Mary.

Now the Old One was calling to her. He was calling
to her in her dream.

The Old One's voice got louder. He was saying,
"Eyes-Looking-Up. Go to the river. Go to the river.
Eyes-Looking-Up, go to the river."

Mary turned over in her sleeping bag again. It was warm
in the tent. But the Old One's voice got louder and louder.
It called, "Eyes-Looking-Up! Go to the river!"

In her dream Mary tried to answer the Old One. It was the sound of her own voice that woke her up. Suddenly, she smelled smoke. The smell was strong. Shadows were dancing against the walls of the tent! A fire had started while she was asleep!

Mary jumped up. She hurried to the opening in the tent. She looked out. A tree was on fire! The wind was **spreading** the fire. Now the fire was eating at everything! It was moving closer to the tents!

"Mary. What is wrong? What is that light?" a sleepy child asked.

"Get up, Sarah!" said Mary. "Hurry! Help me wake up the others!"

Mary pulled the four other children out of their beds. She led them out of the tent. She took them to the center of the camp.

"Fire! Fire!" she yelled, as loudly as she could. "Wake up! Get up!"

Mary ran back to the tent. She grabbed all the sleeping bags she could carry. By then everyone had come out of the tents. The children were **scared**. There was fear on their faces.

Mary took the two youngest children by the hand. She pulled them along. The other children followed her. They held on to each other.

"Mary!" called the leader of the camp. "Put down those sleeping bags! You can't run with them!"

But Mary held on to the sleeping bags. She kept moving. She followed the path. It went down to the river.

There was no time to explain. Mary pulled the children into the water. Then she got into the water. She dragged the sleeping bags in. She pushed them under the water until they were **soaked**.

"Mary! What are you doing!" the camp leader called. "Don't lose your head! Stop moving around!"

Mary pointed to some trees near the river. She said, "Those trees will soon be on fire. The fire will jump over the river. When it does, we must keep our heads under the water. The children will not be able to do that for very long. We *have* to get under the wet sleeping bags! They will keep the heat and the smoke away!"

The leader understood. "Come on," she said to Mary. "Let's go!" They ran back up the path. They went to get more sleeping bags.

Minutes later they came back. They had more sleeping bags. They dropped them into the water. Then everyone waited.

It had been a very hot summer. Everything was dry. The forest burned quickly. Now all the trees were on fire.

Mary looked around. She saw many animals. They were racing to the river. Deer, rabbits, and squirrels splashed into the water.

The fire roared. The flames were coming toward them. Mary could feel the heat on her face.

Mary and the other counselors grabbed the wet sleeping bags. They pulled them over the children's heads. Then Mary called out, "Listen, everybody! Stay down in the water! Keep your mouth just above the water. Leave just enough room for you to breathe. Now, everybody hold hands. Remember. No matter what happens, keep down!"

Mary got under a wet sleeping bag. Just then a wall of flames jumped over the river. Suddenly, Mary felt as if she were in one of her grandfather's stories. She used to get tired of hearing the Old One's stories. He talked on and on. He always talked about the old days long ago.

Mary loved to listen to him when she was young. She knew each story by heart. Later, she got tired of hearing the same stories. But one of those stories might save their lives now!

The Old One had told her one story many times. He had heard the story from his own father. His father's father had once saved a village from a forest fire. He had covered everyone with wet blankets. Then he led the people to the river. The wet blankets **protected** them from the heat.

Her grandfather loved that story. He told it over and over to little Eyes-Looking-Up. When he finished, the Old One always smiled. Then he said, "Never forget the ways of your people."

Mary knew that the sleeping bags would have to stay wet.

She looked up from under her bag. She would never forget what she saw. Everything around them was bright orange and red.

Mary and the other counselors splashed water over all the sleeping bags. They felt the terrible heat on their arms and hands. But they kept the sleeping bags wet. Then they ducked under the bags.

It seemed as though it would never stop. But the heat and smoke finally ended. Mary raised her head. She looked around. Not one of the children was hurt!

"Mary," the camp leader said. "You saved our lives! How did you know what to do?"

Mary smiled. "My grandfather told me in a dream," she said.

She knew then that she would carry on for the Old One. She, too, would be a teller of stories. And one day she would say to her own children, "Never forget the ways of your people."

TELL ABOUT THE STORY.

Put an *x* in the box next to the right answer. Each sentence tells a *fact* about the story.

1. Mary was dreaming about
   - ☐ a. a fire.
   - ☐ b. her job.
   - ☐ c. her grandfather.

2. Mary's family moved to the city
   - ☐ a. to make new friends.
   - ☐ b. to be closer to the school.
   - ☐ c. so that her father could get a better job.

3. Mary used the wet sleeping bags to
   - ☐ a. sleep on.
   - ☐ b. cover the food.
   - ☐ c. keep the heat and the smoke away.

4. At the end of the story, Mary saw that
   - ☐ a. none of the children had been hurt.
   - ☐ b. some of the children had been hurt.
   - ☐ c. all of the children had been hurt.

ADD WORDS TO SENTENCES.

Complete the sentences below. Fill in each blank with one of the words in the box. Each word can be found in the story. There are five words and four blanks. This means that one word in the box will not be used.

Here is what to do if you are ever in a _____ building. Warn
$_1$
others near you about the fire. Then _____ the building at once.
$_2$
Do not go _____ for anything
$_3$
you may have left behind. Call the _____ department as soon as
$_4$
you can.

fire	leave
burning	
pointing	back

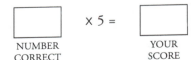

NUMBER CORRECT   x 5 =   YOUR SCORE

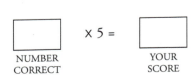

NUMBER CORRECT   x 5 =   YOUR SCORE

121

LEARN NEW WORDS.

The vocabulary words are printed in **dark type** in the story. You may look back at the words before you answer these questions. Put an *x* in the box next to the right answer.

1. The wind was spreading the fire. The word *spreading* means
   - ☐ a. moving.
   - ☐ b. stopping.
   - ☐ c. leaving.

2. They were scared by the fire. The word *scared* means
   - ☐ a. made quiet.
   - ☐ b. made afraid.
   - ☐ c. made sad.

3. She pushed the bags under the water until they were soaked. The word *soaked* means
   - ☐ a. very soft.
   - ☐ b. very heavy.
   - ☐ c. very wet.

4. The wet blankets protected them from the fire. The word *protected* means
   - ☐ a. hurt.
   - ☐ b. pushed.
   - ☐ c. kept safe.

☐ X 5 = ☐

NUMBER CORRECT   YOUR SCORE

EXPLAIN WHAT HAPPENED.

Here is how to answer these questions. First think about what happened in the story. Then *figure out* (work out) the right answer. This is called *critical thinking*.

1. If Mary had not told everyone what to do,
   - ☐ a. campers might have been hurt or killed.
   - ☐ b. they would have stayed.
   - ☐ c. everyone would still have been saved.

2. What was *not* true of the dream?
   - ☐ a. It woke Mary up.
   - ☐ b. It said to go to the river.
   - ☐ c. It was long.

3. Mary learned that it was important to
   - ☐ a. remember the ways of her people.
   - ☐ b. forget the old stories.
   - ☐ c. go to bed early.

4. How often will Mary probably tell the story about the fire?
   - ☐ a. never
   - ☐ b. one or two times
   - ☐ c. many times

☐ X 5 = ☐

NUMBER CORRECT   YOUR SCORE

SPOT STORY ELEMENTS.
Some story elements are **plot,
character,** and **setting.** (See
page 3.) Put an *x* in the box
next to the right answer.

1. What happened first in the *plot*?
   - ☐ a. Mary went back to get
     more sleeping bags.
   - ☐ b. Mary woke up and
     smelled smoke.
   - ☐ c. Mary took the children to
     the river.

2. What happened last in the *plot*?
   - ☐ a. The heat and smoke
     ended.
   - ☐ b. Mary pulled four children
     out of their beds.
   - ☐ c. Animals ran into the water.

3. Who is the *main character* in the
   story?
   - ☐ a. Mary
   - ☐ b. Mary's father
   - ☐ c. The Old One

4. The story is *set*
   - ☐ a. in a school.
   - ☐ b. in the country.
   - ☐ c. in the middle of a city.

THINK SOME MORE
ABOUT THE STORY.
Your teacher might want you to
write your answers.

- Suppose Mary had not been
  working at the camp. How do
  you think the story would have
  ended?
- Who saved the campers—Mary
  or her grandfather or both?
  Explain your answer.
- Read the last lines of the story
  again. How was Mary going to
  "carry on for the Old One"?

Write your scores in the boxes below.
Then write your scores on pages 138
and 139.

☐ + **T**ELL ABOUT THE STORY
☐ + **A**DD WORDS TO SENTENCES
☐ + **L**EARN NEW WORDS
☐ + **E**XPLAIN WHAT HAPPENED
☐ = **S**POT STORY ELEMENTS
☐ TOTAL SCORE: Story 9

☐ × 5 = ☐

NUMBER   YOUR
CORRECT   SCORE

10
The Fight of the Crickets

by Lin Yutang

Before You Read

Before you read "The Fight of the Crickets," study the words below. Make sure you know what each word means. This will help you understand the story.

net: something used to catch things. Most nets are light and have very small holes.

jar: a glass bottle

champion: the best at something

stream: a small river

jaws: the bones that move the mouth up and down

disappeared: could not be seen

The Fight of the Crickets

by Lin Yutang

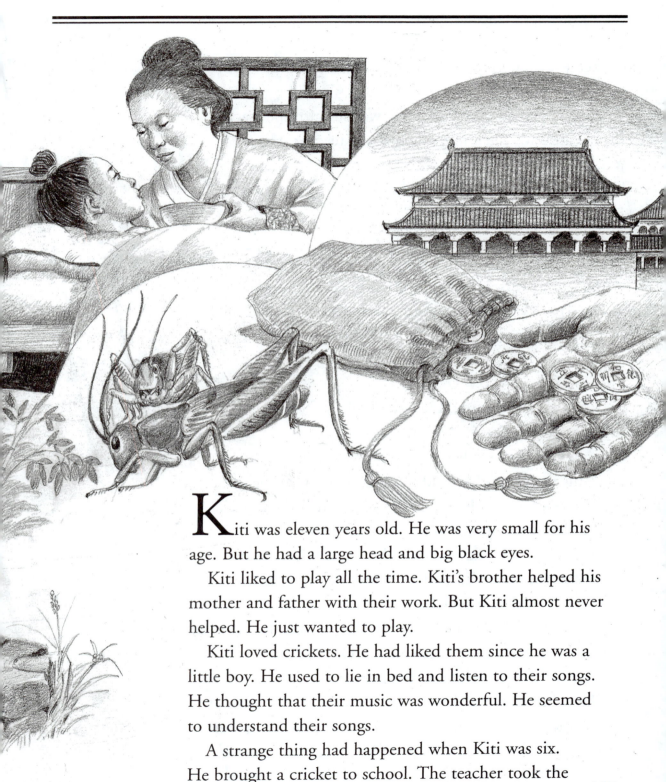

Kiti was eleven years old. He was very small for his age. But he had a large head and big black eyes.

Kiti liked to play all the time. Kiti's brother helped his mother and father with their work. But Kiti almost never helped. He just wanted to play.

Kiti loved crickets. He had liked them since he was a little boy. He used to lie in bed and listen to their songs. He thought that their music was wonderful. He seemed to understand their songs.

A strange thing had happened when Kiti was six. He brought a cricket to school. The teacher took the

127

cricket away. He threw the cricket on the ground. Then he stepped on it.

This made Kiti very angry. He waited until the teacher turned around. Then he **rushed** at the teacher. He jumped on his back. He started hitting the teacher with his small fists. Nothing like that had ever happened before.

One afternoon a wonderful thing happened to Kiti. His father, Mr. Cheng, said, "Kiti, let us catch some crickets today. We can find some in the hills. I will bring a net to catch them. Bring a box to put them in."

Kiti was very excited. He had caught crickets before. But he had never caught them with a net. He had never caught them with his father. And he had never gone up into the hills. There were many crickets in the hills. But the hills were two miles away. He could not go there alone.

It was July. The day was very hot. There were many stones in the hills. Kiti and his father turned over the stones. Then they listened.

They listened for the sound a cricket makes. It is a loud, clear chirp. That chirp tells you a cricket is near. The louder the chirp, the bigger the cricket.

They heard the crickets' chirps two times. But both times the crickets got away. On the way home, Kiti's father was angry. He wanted to catch crickets very much.

Kiti wondered why his father wanted to catch crickets. But Kiti did not ask.

They got back home in the afternoon. His mother was waiting by the door. She asked, "Did you catch any crickets?"

"No," his father said. His father was very sad.

Kiti waited until his mother was alone. Then Kiti said, "Tell me, Mother. Does Father like crickets?"

"No," she said. "He *has* to catch one. He must catch a very strong one. He has ten days to catch one."

"Catch one? Why? For whom?" asked Kiti.

"For the Emperor."

"I do not understand," said Kiti.

"The Emperor likes cricket fights," said his mother. "In July, every village must send a cricket to the Emperor. The crickets fight each other at the palace. The winner gets a lot of money. It is twenty pieces of silver."

Kiti listened with interest.

His mother went on. She said, "This year our Governor picked your father. Your father must **supply** the cricket."

Kiti rushed to his father. "Father," he said, "Mother told me all about the cricket fights! We can catch a good fighter! He could win! He could be the champion of the country!"

Mr. Cheng said, "Could you catch a champion cricket? It would be worth a lot of money."

"Oh, yes!" said Kiti. "Father, we will catch one! It will make us rich!"

Mr. Cheng was glad that Kiti knew a lot about crickets. He was glad that Kiti could help him.

They went out to catch crickets. They looked for two days. They did not find any crickets. On the third day they were lucky. They climbed to the top of a hill. On the other side was a small stream. "Let us look there," said Kiti.

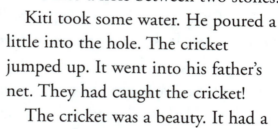

There were some stones in the stream. The stones were large and flat. On the stones were many crickets. They were singing on the stones. One of the crickets was very big. It was the biggest cricket Kiti had ever seen. It had a very loud chirp.

Kiti and his father moved toward the stones. They were very quiet. Suddenly a frog hopped onto the stone. The big cricket jumped up. It went into a hole between two stones.

Kiti took some water. He poured a little into the hole. The cricket jumped up. It went into his father's net. They had caught the cricket!

The cricket was a beauty. It had a long body. It had very strong legs.

"He will be a champion!" said Kiti.

They took the cricket home. They put it in a dark green jar. They made a cover for the jar. It had little holes for air. They put the green jar on a table.

Kiti was very excited. He came into the room often. He liked to hear the cricket chirp.

Then something terrible happened. There was no sound for a long time. Kiti **tapped** the jar. He did not see the cricket move. But it was hard to see inside.

Was the cricket gone? Kiti was worried. He took the jar over to the window. Slowly he took off the top. He wanted to look into the jar.

Suddenly the cricket hopped out. It began to jump around the room. Kiti ran after the cricket. Kiti reached out. He grabbed the cricket! But he grabbed it much too tightly! He broke the cricket's leg! He had hurt the champion cricket!

Kiti was filled with fear. His mouth was dry. He began to cry. Then he ran away from home.

Supper time came. But Kiti had not come back. Mr. Cheng was very angry. He had found the cricket. He saw that the cricket was hurt. Mr. Cheng said, "Kiti is afraid. He must be hiding. But he will come home soon. He will return when he is hungry."

Ten o'clock came. Still Kiti was away. His parents were no longer angry. They were worried. They went out to look for Kiti. It was dark. They took candles so they could see. Finally, they found Kiti. He had fallen into a well. He was lying at the bottom.

Kiti's parents took him home. They put him to bed. They were afraid that he would die.

All night Kiti kept talking in his sleep. He kept saying, "I have killed the champion cricket! I have killed the champion cricket!"

The next day Kiti ate a bit of soup. But the boy had changed. He was very sad. He kept saying, "I have killed the champion cricket."

The family was glad that Kiti was alive. They hoped he would get better. And Mr. Cheng still had four days to catch a cricket. He planned to go back to the stream. He planned to look on the flat stones.

He got up very early. He was just about to leave. Then a strange thing happened. He heard a chirp. It was very loud. He went into the kitchen. He saw a little cricket. It was sitting on the chair.

Mr. Cheng looked at the cricket. He thought, "This cricket is so small. It cannot be a good fighter. But it has a very loud chirp."

Just then the cricket jumped up. It landed on Mr. Cheng's arm. It seemed to want to be caught!

Mr. Cheng looked closely at the cricket. It had a long neck. It had strong jaws. It might be a good fighter. But it was very small. He could not send it to the Emperor. It was much too small!

Just then a neighbor came in. The neighbor owned a large cricket. It was a very good fighter. It had won many fights with other crickets in the village.

The neighbor knew that Mr. Cheng needed a good cricket. The neighbor said, "I will sell you my cricket. But it will cost a lot of money."

Mr. Cheng did not have much money. He could not buy the cricket. So Mr. Cheng said, "I already have a cricket. Look." He showed the neighbor his little cricket.

The neighbor began to laugh. He said, "Do you call that a cricket?"

Mr. Cheng answered, "Then let the two crickets fight."

The neighbor said, "All right."

The two crickets were put into a cage. They stood looking at each other. Suddenly the little cricket moved. It jumped high into the air. It landed on the other cricket's back. It sank its jaws into the big cricket.

The neighbor was afraid that his cricket would be killed. He put his fingers into the cage. He pulled the two crickets apart.

Mr. Cheng was pleased. He said to himself, "I will send this cricket to the Emperor. I will also send a note. It will say, 'This cricket is small. But it is a very good fighter.'"

Mr. Cheng told his wife about the fight. She said, "That cricket **reminds** me of Kiti. Remember when he jumped on the teacher's back."

Mr. Cheng thought about that. Then he said, "That is so."

Kiti was still very sick. He was asleep most of the time. His mother had to push food down his mouth.

This went on for weeks. Then one day Kiti woke up. He said to his mother, "I have won! I have won!"

"What did you win?" she asked.

Kiti did not answer. He turned to his father. Kiti said, "I did not mean to hurt that cricket. I did not mean to break its leg."

"Do not worry," said the father. "I found a better cricket. He was small. But he was a very good fighter. I sent him to the Emperor."

Kiti said, "I feel better now. But my legs hurt. I feel as though I had run for hundreds of miles."

The next day Kiti got up. He was able to walk a little. His parents brought him good food.

Kiti said, "This is like the food I had at the palace."

"Where?"

"At the Emperor's palace."

"You must have been dreaming," said his mother.

"It seems very real," said Kiti. "I remember I had a big fight. It was with a big fellow. Everyone came to watch. It was a hard fight. But I won! I won!"

The next day news came from the Emperor's palace. Mr. Cheng's cricket had won every fight. He was the champion of the country! They were sending Mr. Cheng twenty pieces of silver.

But a funny thing had happened. The little cricket was gone. After the fight, it suddenly disappeared from its cage.

TELL ABOUT THE STORY.

Put an *x* in the box next to the right answer. Each sentence tells a *fact* about the story.

1. Kiti was different because he
   - ☐ a. loved crickets and their songs.
   - ☐ b. helped his family so much.
   - ☐ c. did not like to play.

2. Kiti and his father saw some crickets
   - ☐ a. in the grass.
   - ☐ b. on a tree.
   - ☐ c. on large flat stones.

3. Kiti fell into
   - ☐ a. the river.
   - ☐ b. the well.
   - ☐ c. a stone.

4. The Emperor was sending Mr. Cheng
   - ☐ a. some gold.
   - ☐ b. twenty dollars.
   - ☐ c. twenty pieces of silver.

ADD WORDS TO SENTENCES.

Complete the sentences below. Fill in each blank with one of the words in the box. Each word can be found in the story. There are five words and four blanks. This means that one word in the box will not be used.

In some ways the _____
₁ and the grasshopper are very much alike. Both have _____ back
₂ legs and can jump very far. Both like to eat the same kind of _____.
₃ And both can make _____ by
₄ rubbing the edges of their wings together.

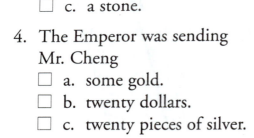

strong   teacher
        cricket
sounds   food

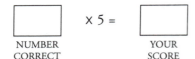 x 5 =

NUMBER CORRECT   YOUR SCORE

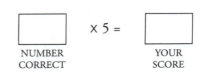 x 5 =

NUMBER CORRECT   YOUR SCORE

135

LEARN NEW WORDS.

The vocabulary words are printed in **dark type** in the story. You may look back at the words before you answer these questions. Put an *x* in the box next to the right answer.

1. Kiti rushed at the teacher and jumped on his back. The word *rushed* means
   - ☐ a. called to.
   - ☐ b. fell down.
   - ☐ c. moved quickly.

2. He had to supply a cricket for the Emperor. The word *supply* means
   - ☐ a. take away.
   - ☐ b. like very much.
   - ☐ c. give what is needed.

3. Kiti tapped the jar. The word *tapped* means
   - ☐ a. hit lightly.
   - ☐ b. threw away.
   - ☐ c. kicked.

4. She said, "That cricket reminds me of Kiti." The word *reminds* means
   - ☐ a. makes you think of.
   - ☐ b. is different from.
   - ☐ c. is smaller than.

☐	× 5 =	☐
NUMBER CORRECT		YOUR SCORE

EXPLAIN WHAT HAPPENED.

Here is how to answer these questions. First think about what happened in the story. Then *figure out* (work out) the right answer. This is called *critical thinking*.

1. Which sentence is true?
   - ☐ a. Kiti did not like crickets.
   - ☐ b. Mr. Cheng loved crickets.
   - ☐ c. Kiti and the champion cricket were alike in many ways.

2. What was strange about the cricket that Mr. Cheng found?
   - ☐ a. It had a long neck.
   - ☐ b. It seemed to want to be caught.
   - ☐ c. It was a good fighter.

3. It is interesting that when Kiti finally woke up, he said,
   - ☐ a. "I feel very tired."
   - ☐ b. "Where am I?"
   - ☐ c. "I won! I won!"

4. The cricket probably disappeared at the end of the story because
   - ☐ a. it had done its job.
   - ☐ b. the Emperor sold it.
   - ☐ c. Mr. Cheng took it.

☐	× 5 =	☐
NUMBER CORRECT		YOUR SCORE

SPOT STORY ELEMENTS.

Some story elements are **plot**, **character**, and **setting**. (See page 3.) Put an *x* in the box next to the right answer.

1. What happened first in the *plot*?
   - ☐ a. Kiti and his father hunted for crickets.
   - ☐ b. Kiti ran away from home.
   - ☐ c. Mr. Cheng's cricket won.

2. What happened last in the *plot*?
   - ☐ a. The family looked for Kiti.
   - ☐ b. Kiti brought a cricket to school.
   - ☐ c. They found out Mr. Cheng's cricket was the champion.

3. Who is the *main character* in the story?
   - ☐ a. the Emperor
   - ☐ b. Kiti
   - ☐ c. Mr. Cheng

4. Which sentence best *characterizes* (tells about) Kiti?
   - ☐ a. He was tall for his age.
   - ☐ b. He never got sick.
   - ☐ c. He was small and had a large head with big eyes.

☐ x 5 = ☐

NUMBER CORRECT   YOUR SCORE

THINK SOME MORE ABOUT THE STORY.

Your teacher might want you to write your answers.

- In what ways were Kiti and Mr. Cheng's cricket alike?
- What did Kiti dream? Why do you think that his dreams seemed so real to him?
- At the end of the story, Kiti felt as though he had run for hundreds of miles. Why? Did you think Mr. Cheng's cricket would be the champion? Explain.

Write your scores in the boxes below. Then write your scores on pages 138 and 139.

☐ **T**ELL ABOUT THE STORY
\+
☐ **A**DD WORDS TO SENTENCES
\+
☐ **L**EARN NEW WORDS
\+
☐ **E**XPLAIN WHAT HAPPENED
\+
☐ **S**POT STORY ELEMENTS
=
☐ TOTAL SCORE: Story 10

Progress Chart

1. Write in your score for each exercise.
2. Write in your TOTAL SCORE.

	T	A	L	E	S	TOTAL SCORE
Story 1						
Story 2						
Story 3						
Story 4						
Story 5						
Story 6						
Story 7						
Story 8						
Story 9						
Story 10						

Progress Graph

1. Write your TOTAL SCORE in the box under the number for each story.
2. Put a *x* along the line above each box to show your TOTAL SCORE for that story.
3. Make a graph of your progress by drawing a line to connect the *x*'s.

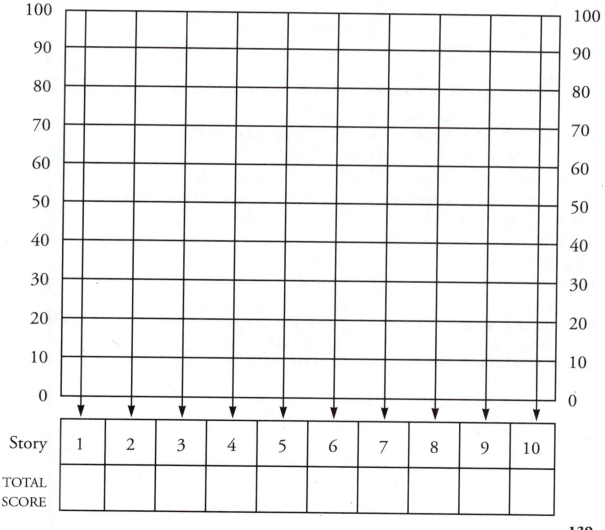

Acknowledgments

Text:
Acknowledgment is gratefully made to the following publishers, authors, and agents for permission to reprint these works. Adaptations, retellings and/or abridgments are by Burton Goodman. All rights reserved.

"The Day It Snowed Tortillas" from *The Day It Snowed Tortillas: Tales from Spanish New Mexico* retold by Joe Hayes. Reprinted by permission of Mariposa Printing & Publishing, Santa Fe, New Mexico.

"The Visitors" by George Shea. All attempts have been made to locate the copyright holder.

"Tea for Two" from *Let Me Read Your Tea Leaves* by Joan Mosby. Reprinted by permission of Larry Sternig/Jack Byrne Literary Agency.

"Anansi and the Sea" based on the story "Thunder and Anansi." Collected in *West African Folk-tales* by W. H. Barker and C. Sinclair. George G. Harrap and Company, London, 1917.

"Fresh Fish Sold Here" by Angel Flores from *First Spanish Reader, A Beginner's Dual-Language Book* by Angel Flores. Copyright © 1964 by Bantam Books, Inc. Reprinted by permission of the Estate of Angel Flores.

"The Fire" by Shirley Nagel. All attempts have been made to locate the copyright holder.

"The Fight of the Crickets" from "The Cricket Boy" by Lin Yutang from *Famous Chinese Short Stories* by Lin Yutang. Copyright © 1948, 1951, 1952 by (John Day Co.) Harper & Row Publishers, Inc. Reprinted by permission of Taiyi Lin Lai and Hsiang Ju Lin.

Illustrations:
David Cunningham
Yoshi Miyake